Giving a Lecture

From presenting to teaching

Kate Exley and Reg Dennick

RoutledgeFalmer
Taylor & Francis Group
LONDON AND NEW YORK

First published 2004 by RoutledgeFalmer
11 New Fetter Lane, London EC4P 4EE

Simultaneously published in the USA and Canada
by RoutledgeFalmer
29 West 35th Street, New York, NY 10001

RoutledgeFalmer is an imprint of the Taylor & Francis Group

Typeset in Perpetua and Bell Gothic by Graphicraft Limited, Hong Kong
Printed and bound in Great Britain by TJ International, Padstow, Cornwall

Key Guides for Effective Teaching in Higher Education web resource

The Key Guides for Effective Teaching in Higher Education Series provides guidance and advice for those looking to improve their teaching and learning. It is accompanied by a useful website which features brand new supplementary material, including How Students Learn, a guide written by Professor George Brown which provides outlines and commentaries on theories of learning and their implications for teaching practice.

Visit the website at: www.routledgefalmer.com/series/KGETHE

The RoutledgeFalmer website also features a wide range of books for lecturers and higher education professionals.

British Library Cataloguing in Publication Data
A catalogue record for this book is available from the British Library

Library of Congress Cataloging in Publication Data
Exley, Kate, 1964–
Giving a lecture : from presenting to teaching / Kate Exley and Reg Dennick.
p. cm.
Includes bibliographical references and index.
1. Lecture method in teaching. I. Dennick, Reg, 1949– II. Title.
LB2393.E95 2004
378.1′796–dc22

2003018375

ISBN 0–415–30718–X (hbk)
ISBN 0–415–30719–8 (pbk)

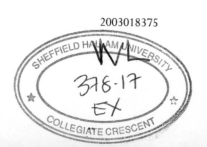

Givi

Thi
edu
adv

Jar
fect
ture
com

■

■
■
■
■

The
sett
grad
any

Kat
and
Dire

Key Guides for Effective Teaching in Higher Education Series

Edited by Kate Exley

This indispensable series is aimed at new lecturers, postgraduate students who have teaching time, graduate teaching assistants, part-time tutors and demonstrators, as well as experienced teaching staff who may feel it's time to review their skills in teaching and learning.

Titles in this series will provide the teacher in higher education with practical, realistic guidance on the various different aspects of their teaching role, which is underpinned not only by current research in the field, but also by the extensive experience of individual authors, and with a keen eye kept on the limitations and opportunities therein. By bridging a gap between academic theory and practice, all titles will provide generic guidance on teaching, learning and assessment issues which is then brought to life through the use of short illustrative examples drawn from a range of disciplines. All titles in this series will:

- represent up-to-date thinking and incorporate the use of communication and information technologies (C&IT) where appropriate;
- consider methods and approaches for teaching and learning when there is an increasing diversity in learning and a growth in student numbers;
- encourage reflective practice and self-evaluation, and a means of developing the skills of teaching, learning and assessment;
- provide links and references to further work on the topic and research evidence where appropriate.

Titles in the series will prove invaluable whether they are used for self-study or as part of a formal induction programme on teaching in higher education, and will also be of relevance to teaching staff working in further education settings.

Other titles in this series:

Assessing Students' Written Work
– Catherine Haines

Small Group Teaching: Tutorials, Seminars and Beyond
– Kate Exley and Reg Dennick

Using C&IT to Support Teaching
– Paul Chin

Contents

Illustrations

Figures

Tables

Series preface

This series of books grew out of discussions with new lecturers and part-time teachers in universities and colleges who were keen to develop their teaching skills. However, experienced colleagues may also enjoy and find merit in the books, particularly the discussions about current issues that are impacting on teaching and learning in further education and higher education (e.g. Widening Participation, disability legislation and the integration of Communication and Information Technology (C&IT) in teaching).

New lecturers may be required by their new institutions to take part in teaching development programmes. This frequently involves attending workshops, investigating teaching through mini-projects and reflecting on their practice. Many teaching programmes ask participants to develop their own teaching portfolios and to provide evidence of their developing skills and understanding. Scholarship of teaching is usually an important aspect of the teaching portfolio. New teachers can be asked to consider their own approach to teaching in relation to the wider literature, research findings and theory of teaching and learning. However, when people are beginning their teaching careers a much more pressing need may be to design and deliver an effective teaching session for tomorrow. Hence the intention of this series is to provide a complementary mix of very practical teaching tips and guidance together with a strong basis and clear rationale for their use.

In many institutions the numbers of part-time and occasional teachers actually outnumber the full-time staff. Yet the provision of formal training and development for part-time teachers is more sporadic and variable across the sector. As a result this diverse group of educators can feel isolated and left out of the updating and support offered to their full-time counterparts. At no time has there been so many part-time teachers involved in the design and delivery of courses, the support and guidance of students and the monitoring and assessment of learning. The group includes the thousands of postgraduate students who work as lab demonstrators, problem class tutors, project supervisors and class teachers. The group includes clinicians, lawyers and professionals who contribute their specialist knowledge and skills to enrich the learning experience for many vocational and professional course students. The group also includes the many hourly paid and jobbing tutors who have helped full-time staff cope with the expansion and diversification of HE and FE.

Universities sometimes struggle to know how many part-time staff they employ to teach and, as a group, occasional teachers are notoriously difficult to contact systematically through university and college communication systems. Part-time and occasional teachers often have other roles and responsibilities and teaching is a small but important part of what they do each day. Many part-time tutors would not expect to undertake the full range of teaching activities of full-time staff but may well do lots of tutoring or lots of class teaching but never lecture or supervise (or vice versa). So the series provides short practical books focusing very squarely on different teaching roles and activities. The first four books published are:–

- *Small Group Teaching*
- *Giving a Lecture: From Presenting to Teaching*
- *Assessing Students' Written Work*
- *Using C&IT to Support Teaching*

The books are all very practical, with detailed discussion of teaching techniques and methods, but they are based upon educational theory and research findings. Articles are referenced, further readings and related websites are given and workers in the field are quoted and acknowledged. To this end Dr George Brown has been commissioned to produce an associated web-based guide on Student Learning which can be freely accessed by readers to accompany the books and provide a substantial foundation for the teaching and assessment practices discussed and recommended in the texts. The URL for this site is: www.routledgefalmer.com/series/KGETHE

There is much enthusiasm and support here too for the excellent work currently being carried out by the Learning and Teaching Support Networks (LTSN) within discipline groupings (indeed individual LTSN centres are suggested as sources of further information throughout these volumes). The need to provide part-time tutors with the realistic connections with their own disciplines is keenly felt by all the authors in the series and 'how it might work in your department' examples are given at the end of many of the activity-based chapters. However, there is no doubt some merit in sharing teaching developments across the boundaries of discipline, culture and country as many of the problems in the tertiary education sector are themselves widely shared.

UNDERLYING THEMES

The use of Computing and Information Technology (C&IT) to enrich student learning and to help manage the workload of teachers is a recurrent theme in the series. I acknowledge that not all teachers may yet have access to state-of-the-art teaching resources and facilities. However, the use of Virtual Learning Environments, e-learning provision and audio-visual presentation media is becoming increasingly widespread in universities.

The books also acknowledge, and try to help new teachers respond to, the growing and changing nature of the student population. Students with non-traditional educational backgrounds, international students, students who have disabilities or special needs are encouraged through the government's Widening Participation agenda to take part in further and higher education (F and HE). The books seek to advise teachers on current legislative requirements and guide on recommended good practice in teaching diverse groups of students.

These were our goals and I and my co-authors sincerely hope these volumes prove to be a helpful resource for colleagues, both new and experienced, in HE.

Kate Exley

Acknowledgements

The authors of this book gratefully acknowledge the support, input and encouragement that they have received from friends, colleagues and family. Particular thanks to George Brown and Richard Blackwell for their guidance and insightful suggestions during the writing of this book.

Steve Draper at the University of Glasgow and David Nicol at the University of Strathclyde are thanked sincerely for their expertise and willingness to share it, on the use of interactive handsets in lectures and their impact on student learning.

The book has been framed with particular people in mind, i.e. the new teachers who have attended our teaching and learning workshops in recent years. Particular thanks are due to the occasional teachers at the London School of Economics (LSE), the medical clinicians at the University of Nottingham and the postgraduates who teach at De Montfort, Warwick and Liverpool universities.

Special thanks must go to colleagues who have given their views and told us about their approaches to lecturing from a wide range of discipline areas. The list is by no means exhaustive but does include Liz Barnett, Liz Sockett, Wyn Morgan, Stan Taylor, Stephen Griffiths, Paul Francis, David Pollack, Peter Mayer, Paul Chin, Peter Davies and Tony Short.

A big thank you to Mike Exley for the original illustrations in the book.

Sincere thanks, too, to Alison Foyle and Priyanka Pathak at RoutledgeFalmer. Their knowledge of the process of writing and publishing and their understanding of authors' foibles made their help and guidance invaluable.

Introduction

Lecturing is the cornerstone of many undergraduate courses and is believed by many academics to be the only way that their subjects can now be taught to increasing numbers of students. Many universities are spending thousands of pounds in refurbishing lecture theatres and up-dating the technological support and the provision of audio-visual equipment to make this form of teaching more effective.

'Lecturer' remains the title of the university and college teacher and many students expect to be lectured to. Teaching timetables, in the main, continue to include the words 'lecture' rather than 'large group session or workshop'. However, many courses have gone through rigorous change in recent times and in some cases the lecture, considered to be outmoded and ineffective, has been removed. However, it is interesting to observe that a couple of years down the line many tutors have ended up reintroducing the lecture into their courses. For example, many problem-based learning (PBL) courses were initially designed and structured to run without lectures but, in some cases, student demand has led tutors to introduce 'plenary' sessions that are essentially lectures.

There is no doubt that we probably overuse lectures in many higher education (HE) courses and some aspects of the curriculum cannot be sensibly 'covered' in a lecture theatre. However, we argue in this book that by clearly considering the strengths and weaknesses of this form of teaching we can help ensure that it is used effectively and not simply used because it is what we have always done (and what was done to us!).

The early chapters focus on the skills and techniques needed to write and deliver material clearly and interestingly. There are many examples of practice and clear advice is given. Much of the latter part of the book is dedicated to improving the lecture. A range of strategies for broadening the learning scope, breadth and depth of the traditional didactic lecture are considered. The emphasis being to support the move from presenting to teaching by encouraging students to participate and engage with the lecture material and thus increase the likelihood that deep learning can take place. This does involve a considerable change in culture and a reappraisal of the lecture from both teachers and students. The authors hope that this volume holds some useful ways forward for many new teachers and maybe a few experienced colleagues too.

In addition to 'Further reading', each chapter ends with a list of useful websites. All websites referred to were functional at the time of going to press.

Chapter 1

Why lecture?

THE HISTORY OF THE LECTURE

The lecture, presented to hundreds of students in a lecture theatre, is the standard model of academic teaching. Academic staff in the UK are called lecturers and readers, terms deriving from the Latin *lectare* meaning 'to read aloud'. The technique goes back many hundreds of years, to the monasteries of Europe before the use of printed books, where scholars would travel hundreds of miles to gain access to specific texts. In a *scriptorium* a monk at a *lectern* would read out a book and the scholars would copy it down word for word. One wonders whether much has changed since then as the activity of copying down the lecturer's notes is still one of the main functions of lecturing in higher education.

> Lecturing is the transference of the notes of the lecturer to the notes of the student without passing through the brains of either.
>
> (Anon)

Traditionally lecturing is often perceived by students as boring, with little intellectual stimulation coming from monotonous lecturers.

> Most people tire of a lecture in ten minutes; clever people can do it in five. Sensible people never go to lectures at all.
>
> (Stephen Leacock in Sherin 1995: 104)

In recent years a great deal of discussion has focused on the development of 'active learning' in higher education (see series website guide, Brown 2004). Lecturing is often viewed as an example of 'passive learning' in which the only activities students engage in during a lecture are listening and note taking. Such lectures are often described as 'didactic' which means 'intending to instruct', from the Greek, *didaskein*, 'to teach'. Active learning on the other hand includes activities such as discussion, questioning, problem solving and other forms of interactivity, which are, traditionally, not carried out during a lecture. As active learning has been shown to encourage deeper learning there has been a move away from lecturing to more small group teaching, self-directed learning and problem-based learning. However, as student numbers have increased in tertiary education and many universities have tried to resist the pressures of increasing staff/student contact hours in order to protect research productivity, there has been a recent increase in lecturing together with other forms of large group teaching. How can these two very different positions be justified? The view supported here is that lecturing need not be passive and that there are a variety of different learning activities that can be carried out by students during a lecture.

LECTURING AND CONSTRUCTIVE ALIGNMENT

The concept of constructive alignment (Biggs 1999b) suggests that a curriculum should have a set of well-defined learning outcomes that are acquired via a set of appropriate learning experiences. The learning that has taken place is then assessed via a set of appropriately valid assessment tools. The whole system is then evaluated via quality assurance processes and modified if necessary, leading to a process model of the curriculum as shown in Figure 1.1.

It is at the level of learning experiences that decisions need to be made about the balance between different types of teaching methods. Different learning outcomes are more appropriately acquired by different learning or teaching methods. Learning outcomes can be categorized in a number of ways. One method is to use Bloom's Taxonomy (Bloom 1956) which for cognitive objectives is shown in Figure 1.2.

A simplified categorization splits knowledge outcomes into three broad categories:

- factual and conceptual understanding
- application and use
- problem solving and evaluation.

The problem is then to decide which categories of outcome are more appropriately gained using the various teaching and learning modalities

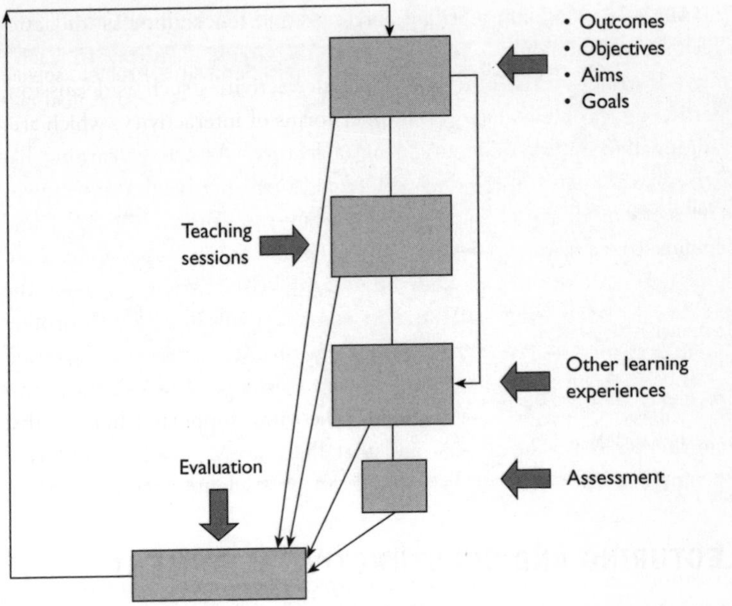

FIGURE 1.1 Constructive alignment

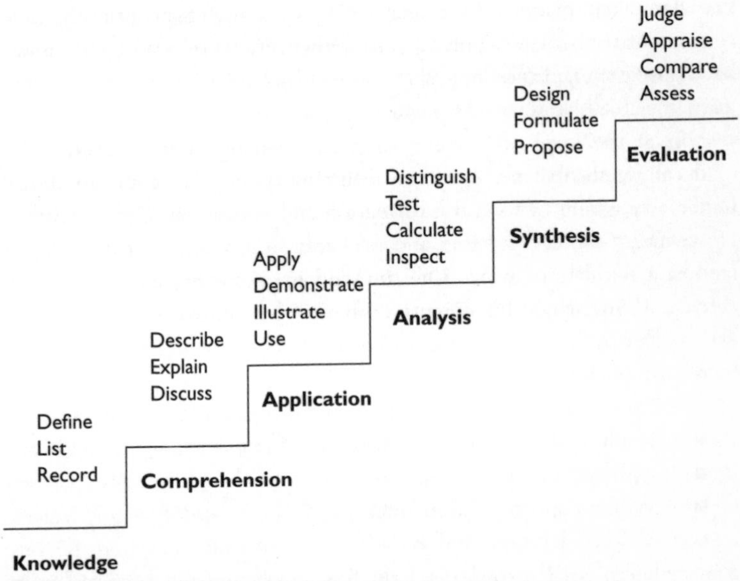

FIGURE 1.2 Bloom's taxonomy for the cognitive domain

TABLE 1.1 Mapping learning outcomes and teaching methods

	Factual and conceptual understanding	Application and use	Problem solving and evaluation
Lecturing	+++	+	+
Small group teaching	+	+++	+++
Self-directed learning	+++	+++	+++
Practicals	+	+++	++
Computer-assisted learning/web	++	+	+
Problem-based learning	++	++	+++
Experiential learning	++	+++	+++

available in higher education. Table 1.1 indicates which of the common modalities are more appropriate for which of the three outcomes.

Some teachers might argue that you can teach application and usage or problem solving and evaluation in lectures. There is no doubt that students in conventional lectures may observe the lecturer engaging in applying knowledge and problem solving and even mentally engaging in the process, so there is some cognitive gain. However, there is a big difference between teaching *about* applying knowledge and problem solving and learners actually applying or problem solving themselves. These activities can be better supported in a small group teaching environment.

It can be seen that *conventional* lecturing appears to be ideally suited to the acquisition of factual information and conceptual understanding. However, it is very possible and probably desirable to create a richer lecturing environment in which the students can carry out a variety of active and interactive learning tasks. It then becomes possible for learners to achieve many of the higher levels of cognitive and skills development within the lecture.

Therefore, constructive alignment suggests that curriculum planners should decide on the balance between different teaching methods and modalities based on the learning outcomes of the curriculum. Clearly key factual and conceptual outcomes will be more appropriately learned in conventional lectures and higher cognitive outcomes may be best acquired in a small group teaching session or partially achieved in an interactive lecture. This situation also raises the question of the relative proportion of key factual and conceptual outcomes there should be in the curriculum in the first place. One of the problems of the modern curriculum, particularly in the scientific and technical disciplines, is the exponential growth in knowledge. This frequently manifests itself as increased facts, ideas and concepts that have to be crammed into an ever-expanding curriculum. But clearly this expansion cannot continue indefinitely. Decisions have to be made on the size of the 'core' factual content of the curriculum and this will clearly influence the number of lectures that will be required.

LEARNING STYLES

Another reason for curriculum planners to include lectures in the curriculum, ensuring a balance with other teaching methods, is the issue of individual learning styles. A number of psychometric tests reveal that learners differ in their approach to learning. For example, Honey and Mumford (1982) suggest that a learner's learning style can be profiled under four categories: activists, reflectors, theorists and pragmatists. The four learning style categories map closely to the four quarters of the experiential learning cycle proposed by David Kolb (1984): concrete experience; observation and reflection; forming abstract concepts, and testing in new situations, and indicate a preference for particular learning activities. For example, learners who are strongly activist in their approach will prefer learning contexts which allow them to 'learn by doing' whereas pragmatists appreciate learning in the light of a clear application and use for their learning. It is important not to use such terminology to 'label' students and to recognize that learning styles are strongly influenced by the learning context and that learners will both challenge and hone their learning preferences during a course of study. (Please see the web-based guide, Brown 2004, for a more detailed discussion of the theories of learning underpinning these learning styles).

A well-known system of personality classification was developed by Kathleen Briggs and Isabel Myers in the twentieth century based on Carl Jung's book *Psychological Types* (Jung and Baynes 1971). The Myers–Briggs Type Indicator reveals a, more complex, set of sixteen categories (Myers–Briggs 2002). David Keirsey has developed and redefined Myers–Briggs terminology and produced the Keirsey Temperament Sorter (KTS) (Keirsey 1998). Here four basic dimensions of temperament are presented: extroversion and introversion; intuition and sensing; thinking and feeling, and judgement and perception. For our purposes these different 'indicator' tests strongly suggest that within a large group of students there will be a distribution of different learning styles and different personality types which encourages the view that our students will learn more or less effectively from different learning situations. On these grounds it is therefore necessary to provide a variety of learning situations so that all students have an opportunity to use their preferred learning style at some time during the course.

COST-EFFECTIVENESS

It is frequently argued that lecturing is the most cost-effective way of teaching students. One lecturer can teach hundreds of students in a large lecture theatre. However, there is a huge conceptual difference between *teaching* students, or 'covering' a topic as it is sometimes referred to, and students *learning* the information presented. If all that was taught was learned then it would be truly cost-effective, but it isn't. Evidence suggests that only 10 per cent of the words delivered in a lecture are recorded in the notes of the students with only a small proportion effectively learned in the short term and with long-term retention significantly reduced (Johnstone and Su 1994). In addition, as previously discussed, the nature of what is learned in conventional lectures is usually only of the factual and conceptual understanding variety; higher cognitive outcomes tend not to be acquired.

However, the arguments surrounding cost-effectiveness usually refer to conventional, passive, didactic lectures; interactive lectures in which the students are encouraged to actively engage with the lecture material, to be described later, can result in a greater level of understanding.

WHAT CAN THE 'TRADITIONAL' LECTURE DO WELL?

The teaching tips given to teachers in the School of Sciences at the University of Staffordshire summarize a commonly held view of the traditional lecture and list the strengths associated with it.

Five reasons for giving lectures

1. **Communicating enthusiasm for the topic**. This is the best reason for delivering lectures as it is one of the few features that cannot be gained by independent learning.

2. **Providing a structure or framework for the material**. A lecture is a good format with which to impose a certain emphasis on the material that students will read about. This might be desirable for a number of reasons. You might wish to emphasize certain points of view (maybe your own), raise issues that will shape the students' thinking about the topic, relate the topic to others in the course, explore practical applications of the central ideas, and so on.
3. **Tailoring material to the students' needs**. Experience might tell you that the textbooks for a topic do not cover the material in sufficient depth or at the right level for your audience. In this case, lectures can serve to 'part digest' the material so that students will be better able to extend their learning using books and other sources. It might also be the case that all of the material you want to cover is not available together in one external source.
4. **Providing current information**. However good the available textbooks and other resources are, they are rarely going to be absolutely up-to-date and, in any case, will not remain so for long. The lecture provides an opportunity to present recent research to students. This may include your own current work or even ideas you have for research that it would be good to conduct.
5. **Using another format is not viable**. This is often the case when you are faced with large student numbers. It is, of course, true that giving a lecture is more cost-effective than repeating a small group seminar a large number of times. However, there may also pedagogic grounds for rejecting other formats.

(Staffordshire University, Teaching and Learning webpages, http://www.staffs.ac.uk/schools/sciences/learning_and_teaching/LTMlect.htm)

THE CRITERIA FOR INCLUDING A LECTURE IN THE CURRICULUM

The discussion above implies that conventional lectures should be focused into particular areas of the curriculum and should only occur when specific conditions are met. The most important are listed and explained below.

Clear overview

- A lecture should be an overview of a key area of knowledge delivered by someone knowledgeable in the field who understands the problems and potential misunderstandings that can occur.
- The lecturer should have refined and processed the information to be presented and should have ensured that it is useful and relevant in terms of overall curriculum outcomes.
- The lecturer should be able to provide added value in terms of simplified explanations of complex concepts that go beyond what might be found in conventional textbook presentations of the subject.
- The lecturer should be aware of the level and stage of the students and should adjust content and explanations appropriately.

Controlled factual content

- The amount of material presented should be strictly controlled and should fit within the overall curriculum outcomes of the course.
- The lecture should focus on the core themes and central arguments and information and should limit the amount of detail and the number and obscurity of examples used.
- If necessary further information can be provided in handouts or in the recommended reading suggested.
- The lecturer does not have to 'cover' everything in the lecture.

Informed and enthusiastic lecturer

- Lecturers should have had some basic training in lecturing and presentation skills and should be competent to use a range of audio-visual aids.
- They should be able to structure and organize a lecture and have good time-management awareness.
- Lecturers should demonstrate enthusiasm for their subject and should communicate this to their audience by means of an interesting and stimulating presentation.

FINAL REMARKS

In summary, then, whether or not you choose to give a lecture should depend on what you are trying to achieve. For the expedient transmission of facts and information then the traditional, expository lecture format is effective. When compared with more discursive forms of teaching there are few possibilities for feedback, student questions and the development of problem solving and higher order cognitive skills (Bligh, 1998). The traditional lecture greatly benefits from being delivered by a knowledgeable, prepared and, above all, enthusiastic teacher. Knowing how to put a message across clearly, structuring material so that learners can follow even the most complex arguments and explanations and using a wide range of audio-visual teaching resources are skills that new teachers need to develop. Early chapters in this book consider many of the practical and theoretical aspects of the development of lecturer abilities in lecturing; see particularly Chapters 2, 4 and 5.

However, the scope of the lecture can be broadened by using 'active learning' strategies and encouraging students to engage more interactively with lecture material, with the lecturer and each other in the lecture theatre. Ways in which this greater student involvement can be achieved are the foci of later chapters in the book, particularly Chapters 6, 7 and 8.

The lecture remains a cornerstone of many teritiary level courses and, due to the increase in students numbers, it is likely to remain so. It doesn't have to be as limited in learning potential as Bligh and others have observed it to be. By blurring the boundaries between teaching formats it is possible to transfer many of the interactive and more discursive teaching strategies to the lecture theatre and expand the range of learning possibilities of the lecture format.

EXAMPLES FROM DIFFERENT DISCIPLINES

Lectures are used in a variety of different ways in the disciplines. Their role and purpose vary depending on their frequency, position and order within a module or course. Here, some examples are given to show how colleagues are using lectures in their teaching and how they see their role changing and developing.

A lecturer in psychology

I was keen to increase the degree of involvement of students in their learning. To this end, I started the course with a number of lead lectures which identified the topic areas and the key research, theory and evaluative issues in each. I then divided the class into a number of small groups, for instance 10 groups of 10 students. I divided the module content into 10 chunks, one for each member of the group. This left each group with a student responsible for each area of the module.

(Dr Paul Sanders, http://ltsnpsy.york.ac.uk/LTSNAsp/tipsbytopictest.asp?Field=IDteachingproblem&searchfor=Large+groups)

Lecturing on the 'Arts Today' module

. . . (there) came (about) a re-visioning of the possibilities of the lecture form itself. Together each guest lecturer and I sought to rework the 'talking head' mode of delivery. We realized that with two of us time-tabled during the lecture we could turn a monologue from one of us into a dialogue between two of us and between the lectern and the auditorium. The 'other' person could seek clarification, question an assumption, read a piece of text, summarize an argument or directly challenge the presenter.

(Haseman, in Edwards, Smith and Webb 2001: Chapter 7)

Active summarizing in a geography lecture

It is good practice for lecturers to summarize their previous talks at the start of a fresh lecture. This places the current lecture in context and can remind students of key issues and points that need to be cross-referenced with the topic(s) about to be covered. It has been suggested that this opening period can be used to stimulate student interest through discussion of either the students' own understanding of the material to be lectured upon or by reviewing some previous work or activity . . . (*students can be asked to undertake this review process for themselves*) . . . Students were formed into groups of four to eight. One student from each group prepared a written review of the previous lecture on a single sheet of paper that is presented to the rest of the group at the start of the next class for a period of three minutes. A further three minutes is devoted to group discussion. The sheet, annotated with new points, is then given to the lecturer.

(Clive Agnew, Geography, Earth and Environmental Sciences subject centre, http://www.glos.ac.uk/gdn/abstracts/a117.htm)

Feeling the constraints in curriculum design in history

. . . limits on course planning were set by a desire not to increase staff contact hours nor to increase the number of seminar room bookings . . . They mean that we have had to have recourse to far more lecture sessions than we felt desirable measured against the goals of the course. However, learning from the approaches developed elsewhere and in educational literature, we incorporated into the course design suggestions, models and guidelines to encourage lecturers to develop interactive elements and sub-sessions within the large-lecture format. Lectures, therefore, still remain a prominent element of the course, comprising 50 per cent of staff/student contact.

(Barker *et al.* 2000)

FURTHER READING

Biggs, J. (1999) 'Enriching large-class teaching', in *Teaching for Quality Learning at University*. Buckingham: Society for Research into Higher Education and Open University Press.

Bligh, D. (1998) *What's the Use of Lectures?* Exeter: Intellect Press.

Horgan, J. (1999) 'Lecturing for learning', in H. Fry, S. Ketteridge and S. Marshall (eds) *A Handbook for Teaching and Learning in Higher Education. Enhancing Academic Practice*. London: Kogan Page.

Light, G. and Cox, R. (2001) *Learning and Teaching in Higher Education. The Reflective Professional*. London: Paul Chapman Publishing.

USEFUL WEB SITES

http://www.gla.ac.uk/services/tls/STAFF/ras/ELPwebpage/project/ Effective Lecturing project is a collaboration between three universities in Scotland (Queen Margaret University College, University of St Andrews,

University of Glasgow). The project aims to develop a set of educational development resources which will be used to support lectures.

http://keirsey.com/ David Keirsey's site offering the free 'Keirsey Sorter' to discover your own personality type.

http://www.ku.edu/~cte/resources/teachingtips/lecturing.html Strengths and weaknesses of the lecture approach explained to new teachers at University of Kansas.

http:www.lgu.ac.uk/deliberations/lecturing/urls.html The 'DeLiberations' site at London Guildhall University: page of links to lecturing sites.

http:www.staffs.ac.uk/schools/sciences/learning_and_teaching/LTMlect.htm The School of Sciences, University of Staffordshire outlines the reasons for and against lecturing.

Chapter 2

Preparing to lecture

INTRODUCTION

Very few new teachers are given whole new courses or modules to design, organize and facilitate. The norm is that a teaching assistant or postgraduate student will be asked to give a number of lectures in a pre-existing course. Clinicians and other professional and specialist contributors are likely to be asked to work as a 'guest lecturer' and provide input on a series of given topics. This chapter assumes this 'contributing to a course' starting point.

FINDING OUT MORE

> Hi Jim, we were talking last month about how it would be really good for your CV if you were able to give a few lectures during your post-doc. Well, later this semester I am scheduled to give a lecture on fungal genetics to the third years. Do you fancy doing it? They're a nice lot and I know this is your area.

This seems to be a reasonably common starting point for many new 'lecturers'. A first reaction may be 'Do I know enough about fungal genetics?' Feeling confident in the material and the content of the lecture is clearly important but it is rarely the most important consideration. The chances are the new lecturer already knows a lot about the topic and may only need to update or add detail and examples to his or her current knowledge.

The challenge is more likely to be in dovetailing the lecture with the rest of the course and integrating the ideas and information to be

TABLE 2.1 What is the lecturing context? Key questions to ask

Questions about the learning context

1. The lecture in the course

- How does the lecture fit within the course/module structure?
- Why is the lecture format appropriate to the learning goals?
- What other forms of teaching are used on the course?
- How is the course assessed?

2. The students in the lecture

- What do your students know already?
- What are your students expecting?
- How else are your students studying, e.g. in seminars, from reading lists?
- How will the students use, or be assessed on, what you teach?

3. The content of the lecture

- What are the learning outcomes for your session?
- How much flexibility do you have to select material, e.g. reading lists, examples etc?
- What comes immediately before and after the lecture(s) you give?
- Does the lecture content relate directly to other classes, e.g. seminar, laboratory or problem classes?

presented with the rest of the students' learning. Table 2.1 suggests a series of useful questions that can help you find out more about the learning context in which you are being asked to operate.

In essence the four key issues to be considered when preparing to present a lecture are:

- **The content**
  To be confident and enthusiastic about the material and ideas to be presented
- **The audience**
  What do the audience know already, what are they interested in and what do they need or want to get from the lecture? How many students will be attending?
- **The presenter's goals**
  What does the presenter wish to communicate, what are the priorities, what are the learning aims and outcomes? How does the lecture relate to assessment?

FIGURE 2.1 'Oh dear, did somebody book the small lecture theatre again?'

- **The learning environment**
  What is the lecture theatre/teaching room like, what facilities and equipment are available and is the lecturer confident in their operation?

SOURCES OF BACKGROUND INFORMATION

A good source of background information is often the course documentation, e.g. module handbooks, course descriptors and validation documents etc. These should clearly describe the learning aims and outcomes of the course and class sessions. Documents should also outline the learning and assessment approaches used on the course.

Programme specification documents (QAA 2000) will detail the overall programme aims and outcomes for the degree or diploma your students are studying. So you can also *see* the bigger picture of what your students are studying and learning.

Conversations with the module convenor, or members of the teaching team responsible for the course, will also help provide information about the student cohort, their level and previous experience. The person who gave the lecture last year may be available to consult and if so it is likely that he or she would be willing to lend you their lecture notes (indeed, a version of these may have been made available electronically to the students in the past).

The module leader/designer will also be best able to guide you on issues of content flexibility and the required links with other teaching sessions, such as related seminars. What is the philosophy of the course, what are the strands that link elements together and what are the sequences of ideas and information that move through the module?

It can also be helpful to try and see the course from the students' perspective. By looking at reading lists, handout material or online resources, a 'guest lecturer' can begin to build up a picture of the experiences of the student. It may also be possible to sit in on the previous lecture or talk to a small group of students about their work on the course.

How are the students going to be assessed? Many strategically motivated students will be very focused on the summative assessments of the course. Do the students have ongoing course work assessments that could impact on the way they perceive the lecture? What form do the final examinations take? If the students are assessed on their ability to understand and disseminate facts and information then it is likely that they will apply the same criteria when judging the value of your lecture. However, an exam focusing on problem solving or interpretation of ideas will lead the students to value the role-modelling of these skills and abilities in the lecture.

THINKING ABOUT CONTENT

The aim of this section is to convince new teachers that they already know most of what they will eventually communicate in their lecture. This, together with the knowledge that if teachers spend three days researching for a lecture they give themselves an horrendous job of reduction when it comes to preparing a fifty-minute lecture on their gathered material. This leads directly to the most common fault made by new lecturers: *having too much to say and running out of time*.

It is also probably accurate to assume that new teachers rarely have three days spare to prepare for every lecture they give. Therefore, purely on the grounds of workload management, it is vital to be very focused in the preparation of a lecture, particularly when it comes to researching the topic. New teachers like to feel very well prepared and may well feel vulnerable if they can't answer every conceivable question on a topic. While thorough preparation is no doubt a good thing, teachers are definitely not expected to be living oracles and the chances are the new teacher completely underestimates their own current abilities, understanding and knowledge base.

THINK OF STRUCTURE AND CONTENT TOGETHER

When planning a lecture it can be very useful to sketch out ideas of the content while beginning to formulate views on the overall structure of the talk. It is too simplistic to suggest that a teacher should research the content, structure the content, prepare lecture notes, produce visual aids and learning resources, rehearse and then give the lecture. Decisions about structuring the lecture and selecting the appropriate content are more often taken together, with one influencing the other.

Plan to give a lecture, for example, next week on safety at your university/college. It will be a fifty-minute, introductory level lecture to first-year undergraduates. Thinking about the content of that lecture it may be appropriate to consider first what might be the key topics to include (Figure 2.2).

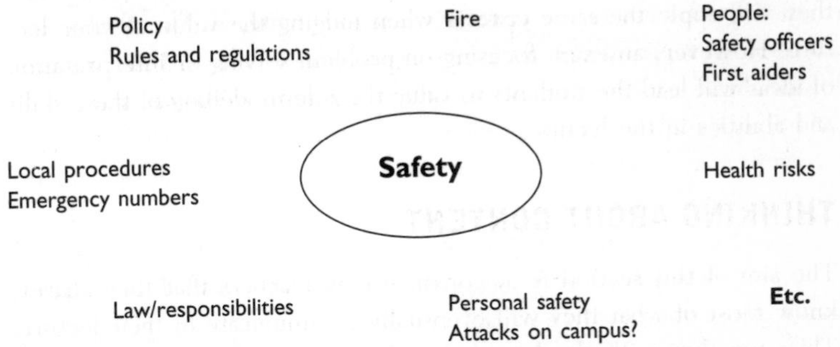

FIGURE 2.2 Suggested key topics to include in a first-year lecture on safety

Having spent about ten minutes noting down sub-topics it may then be helpful to begin to explore different ways in which you could organize and structure the information. Begin to think about where to start and how to grab attention. This is likely to be linked to what you think the students know already and what they need to know by the end of the lecture. Think about the flow and sequencing of one idea to the next. Identify the key messages that the students should prioritize and focus on. How many topics can be covered in the time available and, therefore, what might be grouped together or highlighted? Too much detail and too many topics will detrimentally affect students' learning (Russel, *et al.* 1984).

This interrelationship between content and structure can lead to completely different lectures on exactly the same material. For example, the lecture on safety could begin with a consideration of the law and university regulations, moving on to provide lists of people who have special responsibilities for health and safety and then concluding with a description of the local emergency procedures. Alternatively, a lecture could begin with a question to the students, 'How many ways could you have an accident in this lecture theatre?', or 'What are the potential dangers faced by students studying chemistry at university?', moving on to consider how those hazards could be avoided, managed or responded to, who at the university could help the students and what the regulations and the law say on particular issues.

The same key points can be presented and the same documents and teaching resources used but the two lectures would be experienced very differently by the attending students.

Barbara Gross Davis suggests that it is helpful to

> distinguish between essential and optional material. Divide the concepts or topics you want to cover into three groups: basic material should be mastered by every student, recommended material should be mastered by every student seeking a good knowledge of the subject, and optional material should be mastered by those students with special interests and aptitudes. Lectures and exams should focus on the basic elements of the course. Recommended and optional topics, labelled as such for students, can be included in lectures, supplementary materials, and readings.
>
> (Barbara Gross Davis, http://www.hcc.hawaii.edu/intranet/committees/FacDevCom/guidebk/teachtip/prepcors.htm)

FIGURE 2.3 'Now, what was I writing a lecture on?'

THE PROCESS OF PREPARATION

Through practice and experience teachers find ways of writing and preparing their lectures that work for them. There is no one 'right way' and linear methods are rarely followed absolutely. However, when starting out it can be helpful to have a suggested model to work from.

Preparing a lecture – a personal approach

This is an approach to lecture preparation adapted through experience from ideas originally provided by George Brown (see Brown and Atkins 1988 and Brown and Manogue 2001).

- Spend no more than half an hour reading one or two introductory-level texts or review articles on the lecture topic to refresh the memory and help begin to identify the important branches and sub-topics of the subject.

- Sketch out the themes of the lecture. Use lists or diagrams to group items and points and begin to think about sequencing material and the links between and interrelationship of ideas.
- Decide what you want the student learning outcomes to be. What will the students be able to do when they walk out of the lecture theatre at the end of the lecture that they couldn't do before?
- Decide upon a lecture 'structure' (see Chapter 4) and calculate how much time you wish to spend on each sub-topic. Think about student attention and plan to include learning activities and a variety of experience for the students. Draw up a draft running order for the lecture that begins to include time estimates and a note of the learning resources to be used.
- Draw up a 'shopping list' of specific details and gaps in your knowledge that you would like to include in the lecture and research and read in order to find the information that you need. Try not to get bogged down with too much detail. Look for good illustrative and relative examples. Review and make any changes to the lecture running order – have you forgotten any major themes, etc.?
- Build the lecture by preparing the lecture notes, learning resources, visual aids, online materials etc.
- Look for attention hooks, work in attention grabbers, examples, personal anecdotes, research data etc.
- Plan student activities and learning tasks, such as questions, problems, buzz groups etc. (see Chapter 6) in detail. Include estimates of time and think through the ways that you will give instructions to the students about what you want them to do and why you want them to do it and how you will take feedback etc.
- Finalize the running order sheet and the lecture notes ready to give the lecture.
- How are you going to evaluate your performance and your effectiveness? (See Chapter 10.)

USING CONTACT TIME WELL

The average student's attention span is probably less than twenty minutes in a lecture (Johnstone and Parcival 1976). It is therefore useful to think of preparing a lecture that limits the formal input from the lecturer to ten to fifteen-minute chunks interspersed with breaks or individual and group-based learning activities.

For the first five minutes or so the class will be settling into the lecture room and into the new topic. They will be orientating themselves by remembering what has gone before in the course and thinking of the learning outcomes for today's lecture. The teacher can aid this settling-in process by outlining the topic to be addressed and linking it to previously covered material. It is also helpful if the teacher can give the students the conceptual framework and lecture structure that they will be using, either verbally or in a handout.

Most lecturers also note that their students can concentrate better in the first half of the lecture than in the second half. So plan to explain the most complicated issues or difficult points earlier rather than later in the lecture. (See Chapter 4 for more about how to structure and organize lectures.)

'NOT REALLY MY AREA'

On occasions new teachers may be asked to give a lecture on a topic which they feel is outside their main area of expertise. Here the inclination is very strong to spend a considerable amount of time researching the topic to buoy confidence. However, rarely do we know nothing about a topic we are asked to teach and so taking stock before leaping into research can be just as useful. Consulting an expert may also help in identifying the most important points to consider in the lecture and help steer further reading and research to avoid wasting preparation time.

One reward for the additional work required in these circumstances is that teachers often give a 'better' lecture when they are able to see the subject from the student's perspective. When lecturing on a topic that you know very well, such as your research project, it is very difficult to remember what you once found difficult about the subject. It becomes very hard to empathize with a novice to the field and, therefore, very difficult to pitch the level of a lecture appropriately.

IN CONCLUSION

When preparing lectures it pays to be strategic and use time sparingly. It is so easy to read and research more than is necessary and to end up with far too much to say. This chapter has suggested a number of ways to streamline and make the use of preparation time more efficient. However, every teacher tackles this job in a slightly different way. It can be very useful to keep a note of the hours you spend and briefly describe how you are spending them when you are preparing your next lectures. This is often extremely illuminating and can help you to find the approach that suits you best and develop your own time management strategies.

EXAMPLES FROM DIFFERENT DISCIPLINES – HOW DO YOU PREPARE?

Preparing for a mathematics lecture

Lectures provide the backbone for the module in defining the extent of topics to be covered, the level of study, and the mathematical approach to be adopted – for example whether fundamental concepts are being explored or mathematical techniques developed. A suggested framework for preparing lectures for a module is:

- Familiarization with the content and delivery of an existing module you are taking over, or similar module if new; obtain previously used lecture notes, example sheets and past examination papers.
- Study carefully the module requirements (e.g. module submission document), any existing schedule of topics and their weightings in terms of lecture hours; create a schedule of topics (with approximate lecture hours) and clearly identify any structural changes you envisage. Check with prerequisite modules on what knowledge and skills you might expect students to have and which you will need to cover or review. Check what outcomes, if any, are needed for follow-on modules.
- For each major topic, sketch out your lecture notes, examples to be used for illustrations and examples for students to work through.

- Handouts – decide and prepare materials that you may use within or to support the lecture; these may include
  - complete sets of notes
  - notes giving definitions, theorems and examples
  - summaries of important points and formulae
  - references to standard text or other sources
  - solutions of examples (outline or fully worked).
- Lecture – decide how to deliver the lecture; look for variation in approach and pace, and the types of interaction you might expect the students to participate with. Detailed suggestions within the context of mathematics are provided by Mason (2002: 39–69).

A lecturer preparing to give a lecture on study skills to new first year students

When I'm faced with a totally new topic to lecture on (new to me and not 'knowingly' taught to this group in this context before), I look carefully at the objectives, at the group (and in particular at their vocational or other possible interests). I then do a quick brainstorm of anything that might be useful, interesting, relevant, important, or that just happens to pass through my head at the time. I then look at how the various bits 'fit' – with each other, with the objectives, with the group. And I think about time available. At this stage I might try to boil the ideas down to a few essentials (not more than four or five). Then I'll work out from there on the detailed planning. I might well want to read a bit more, follow up on things I'm not sure of, see if I can get a more appropriate angle for the group. I'd also do more checking on the context (especially if it's a 'one off' slot with students I don't know) – what are the students used to? What comes before/after (both in terms of the actual day, and that course)? Then (in an ideal world) I'd do the detailed preparation at least a couple of days before the actual lecture. (More often, it's the night before.) Then 'let the ideas mature' . . . I find that once I've got the main work done, it's best to leave it quietly simmering in the back of my mind. It's often in this next period that the best ideas come that will bring things to life. An hour or two before the 'live' session I'll then revisit what I've prepared, put in a few 'stage directions' on my notes, and the new ideas (usually in pen + highlighter, rather than changing the PowerPoint or OHPs etc.), and hope for the best!

Right after the session, and in the following twelve hours is when I get the best ideas for redoing a session again another time. To 'hold on' to these ideas I now have a system of using the first slide in the PowerPoint, or first lines of the main document I've used for the session to capture the ideas – so they are there for next time.

(Dr Liz Barnett, Head of the Teaching and Learning Centre, LSE, personal communication)

Preparing a microbiology lecture

For a topic that is not close to my research, I begin ideally a couple of months (and often only a couple of weeks!) beforehand by considering the scope of the topic, the previous relevant knowledge and level of the students and how the two dovetail (if at all). To get fully familiar with the topic I search for both good reviews and key seminal articles usually from the last five years. In my area the former are found in *Trends*, *Current* and *Annual Reviews* (in *Genetics, Biochemistry and Microbiology*) the latter are found in *Nature*, *Science*, *PNAS* and *Molecular Microbiology*. For a three-hour morning module session to final year undergraduates I might read about four reviews and four seminal papers to get me going. These will usually highlight a further dozen papers which I will use to get the primary evidence and experimental detail. They often also lead me into interesting but peripheral disciplines, like immunology. Here I have to decide whether the 'medical interest' makes it worth adding the complexity of diverse science to the lecture.

I begin to draft out a PowerPoint skeleton with key milestones in the topic, drawing figures and inserting pictures of relevant samples. I try to concentrate firstly on areas of the topic where strong experimental lines of evidence show robust and well-accepted mechanisms. This gives the students something concrete to hang their learning on. Once this is done then I may weave in a few controversial areas or topics where the data hasn't yet caught up with the possible ideas. There has to be a balance between key facts and interesting imponderables that is heavily weighted towards the former. If so then the students will feel happy that 'they have plenty to learn for the exam' and will discuss the imponderables. If not then they will fret that 'nothing is certain or worked out at all' and I would have chosen too cutting edge a topic for a lecture class. As the PowerPoint skeleton develops I look out for areas where basic knowledge of the class may be thin. This is usually due to the diversity of the degree backgrounds in the class or the fact that the students haven't been back to a topic since first year. I remedy this by adding a basic figure used in first-year lectures to the presentation, just so everyone can assimilate the new knowledge versus their background. Once I get to the end I review the slides to see if they make sense in their current order, sometimes the order in which things were discovered is confusing and the whole topic needs teaching from the position of hindsight not chronological discovery. At this point I probably have about fifty slides for a total of 2.5 hours lecturing (split by coffee breaks!). I write the summary and the aims and objectives slides at this stage, and also look for any gory or historical slide about ancient plagues that I can add to enliven the subject.

PowerPoint slides are made available on the intranet at my university but the students require and demand paper handouts to annotate while lectures are being delivered. This is where the legibility of diagrams and data rears its ugly head! At this stage I print off a single A4 b/w of each slide and check the legibility. Then to save trees I photocopy-reduce these to two per page double-sided handouts; this makes for a larger and more legible version than using PowerPoint to print two slides per page in handout format as there is less blank space. This will have all taken me a substantial number of hours (estimated at least twelve hours per hour of teaching at this level) but the good thing is that it can all be readily revamped and updated (as in my area it will need every year!) once laid down.

I confess that when developing brand new topics for classroom only teaching from scratch at senior student level I usually 'straight lecture it' for the first year or so to see how the subject goes down before trying to design interactive student-centred learning activities. I hold Question & Answer sessions at the end of the lecture to gauge its effect and ask for shows of hands i.e. understanding as I go through 'hard parts'.

Although preparing lectures from areas at the edge of my scientific discipline is hard work it usually delivers the best to the students in terms of understandability as I've had to learn the area myself and can see where they might have difficulty . . . If I get it then so can they!!

(Dr Liz Sockett, Senior Lecturer in Genetics, personal communication)

A senior lecturer in economics

My initial thoughts when preparing a lecture are based on three questions. How long is the lecture? Which student group forms the audience? What material is required? The first two are easy to answer but clearly shape how the last is answered. To answer it, I ask a further question: what do I want the students to leave the lecture with? If it is simply a framework of knowledge or ideas then that might lean my thinking towards preparing a 'traditional' lecture where I provide guidance through the appropriate material. That of course will require more direct input from me and more material.

If, on the other hand, I want them to develop a means of working something out (for example, mathematical or statistical problems) then a more interactive session needs to be planned with greater emphasis on periods for them to practise the ideas outlined. Here the need is to prepare materials, such as worksheets, that students can work on in the lecture. This requires greater preparation time prior to the lecture although does reduce direct input from me within the lecture. The desired outcomes therefore will shape the nature of the delivery of the lecture.

One point I would offer at this stage is not to ignore the obvious. I do check that the lecture theatre is equipped with the audio-visual aids I need – I have turned up with a PowerPoint presentation before only to find no computer. I also check that I can get materials produced and photocopied in time – I have too many painful memories of colleagues swearing at broken down photocopiers at 8.57 am when they have a 9.00 am lecture!

A wider point to consider is that the lecture I give is unlikely to be a stand-alone experience. As such, what type and range of materials and activities can the students expect after the lecture? Here I try to link back to the original module outline, the recommended reading therein and also to extensions of this such as web sites, *Economist* articles and so forth. Remember, there might also be small group activities to support the lectures. I often deliberately leave out material in the lecture so that it can be covered in the seminar/tutorial that follows. The main purpose of this is to provide a clear link between the lecture programme and support teaching. This, however, requires that I communicate with the tutors for the module, again emphasizing the value of preparation.

One thing I have done to help me in preparing lectures is to keep a teaching 'diary'. When I began lecturing I felt I was bound to make mistakes so I decided to record what I did in lectures, including what material was covered, and then reflected on what worked and what did not. Over the years this has developed to include my teaching aims for each session as well. Again, it is a simple thing to do but I have found it invaluable in updating my teaching each session and in developing my own skills of reflection.

Finally, one point to remember – when writing and giving a lecture, just think back to some of the worst ones you had as a student and think why they did not work for you. Learning from and avoiding the mistakes of others is no bad thing!

(Dr Wyn Morgan, Chair of Teaching and Learning Committee, The University of Nottingham, personal communication)

FURTHER READING

Bligh, D. (1998) *What's the Use of Lectures*, 2nd edition. Exeter: Intellect.

Brown, S. and Race, P. (2002) 'Before and after lectures', in *Lecturing: A Practical Guide*. London: Kogan Page.

Gibbs, G. and the course team (1998) *Practice Guide 2. Lecturing*. H851, Teaching in Higher Education Institute of Educational Technology. Milton Keynes: The Open University.

USEFUL WEB SITES

http://www.northwestern.edu/graduate/TAHandbook/III/lectures.html#preparing TA Handbook (1990) *Conducting Classroom Situations: Lectures*. Evanston, IL: Northwestern University.

http://teaching.berkeley.edu/bgd/largelecture.html Gross Davis, B. (1993) *Preparing to Teach the Large Lecture Course: Tools for Teaching*. Berkeley, CA: University of California.

Chapter 3

Handling nerves, anxieties and discipline problems

INTRODUCTION

Lecturing to large groups of students can cause the adrenaline to rush in the most experienced of lecturers and for the new teacher the prospect can cause anxiety or even fear. This aspect of lecturing often receives very little attention but when considering the skills needed to give a good lecture it is clearly important. Gardner and Leak (1994) identified public speaking as the most common trigger of teaching anxiety. Therefore some ideas about how to manage nerves and control their impact on your effectiveness to teach are discussed here.

Closely associated with increases in lecturer anxiety are fears that the students may behave badly and, although still relatively uncommon, discipline problems, particularly in large lectures, do seem to be on the increase. So this chapter also looks at issues of discipline in the lecture and considers ways of avoiding and dealing with these problems.

NERVES AND ANXIETIES

For most of us this isn't a case of getting rid of our nerves but bringing their effects under control. Some of the world's greatest performers admit to suffering from stage fright, even though they have appeared on stage thousands of times, but their audiences are completely unaware of the fact. It is well documented that university teachers also feel high stress and anxiety levels associated with their teaching activities (Blix *et al.*, 1994). The knowledge that you are not alone and that it is perfectly understandable and 'normal' to feel nervous may help – a little.

Some trainers in public speaking also claim that the slightly flushed face and sparkling eyes of the 'reasonably' nervous speaker can actually

TABLE 3.1 Common symptoms of nerves

When anxious or nervous it is common to experience:

- dry mouth
- sweaty hands
- cold hands
- trembling fingers and hands
- nausea and butterflies in the stomach
- heart racing
- shaky knees
- blushing
- stuttering and jumbling words.

heighten their attractiveness – which may help a little too? However, the same cannot be said for a shaking, blotchy, sweaty and stumbling presenter, so there must be moderation in all things.

People do react very differently to their nerves and the starting point for many new teachers in learning how to handle theirs is to 'know themselves'. What happens to you when you get pre-'stage fright'? It may be that you experience some of the common symptoms of anxiety given in Table 3.1.

REASONS FOR ANXIETY

There are several commonly cited reasons for feeling nervous about presenting or lecturing. The main ones are:

- **Lack of confidence**
  Will those in the audience know more about the topic; are others better presenters?
- **Strange place to be**
  Most people do not spend a great deal of time speaking formally in front of others. It is not part of everyday experience to stand in front of two hundred students in a tiered lecture theatre.
- **Sense of vulnerability**
  You are up there alone and are the centre of attention; the audience may be judging your 'performance'. When put this way it would be unusual if you didn't feel a little exposed and isolated.

- **Feeling self-conscious**
  You may feel shy about your accent, the pitch of your voice or your image more generally.
- **Fear of making mistakes**
  Many speakers worry that they will forget what they wanted to say, or stumble over their words. You may worry about not wishing to offend people, using politically incorrect language or just saying the 'wrong' thing.

STRATEGIES FOR CONTROLLING NERVES

Controlling nerves generally involves two simple strategies; hiding their effect and reducing their symptoms.

Hiding the effects of nerves may, for example, involve the following:

- If your mouth goes dry take in a glass of water to sip. Still water at room temperature is better than ice-cold sparkling water (which can trigger coughing and hiccups).
- If you know your neck always flushes scarlet when you are anxious or embarrassed wear loose comfortable clothing that covers this.
- If you know your hands shake don't hold sheets of A4 paper notes that amplify the tremble.

While reducing their effects could involve:

- developing breathing techniques to calm anxieties and help with butterflies and hammering hearts
- eating a small amount to avoid nausea
- practising the start of the lecture thoroughly to avoid muddles and stutters.

However, there is much that can be done to reduce the sources of anxiety.

BEFORE THE LECTURE

Aim to be kind to yourself and remove as many of your causes for concern as possible. Be comfortable in the lecture theatre, know how to use the equipment provided, organize your teaching materials and notes systematically and be confident in your preparation and knowledge of the subject content.

Find a way of preparing and practising your lecture that helps you. There are no hard and fast rules but you may like to:

- learn your introduction
- practise without your notes using key words or visual aid prompts
- rehearse in front of a mirror
- have a full run-through of the lecture in the teaching room or lecture theatre by yourself
- ask a friend to watch a 'dry run' and give you feedback
- video yourself.

I actually talk to myself in the car driving into work. Although I do get the odd strange look from other drivers at traffic lights it really helps me to formulate easy sentences to say and to plan my opening remarks.

(Teaching assistant in biology)

It is also helpful to find out as much as you can about your student audience. What are their interests and motivations? What are their likely concerns and difficulties? Are you likely to get disruptive students, latecomers or interruptions? Have you thought through how you might handle any of these difficulties if they occurred?

TAKING SOME OF THE PRESSURE OFF

It can also be helpful to remind yourself of the purposes of the lecture. You are up there trying to help your students learn, not to give an Oscar-winning performance. You are trying to communicate with your students. You are having a conversation with them and in conversation people regularly make mistakes and correct themselves, continuing without causing any major impact at all. If you can rethink your 'lecturing role' from being one of 'public speaking' to that of having a conversation with your students, you are likely to be less pressured and you will probably express yourself more freely.

If you feel that you are a particularly shy person or the thought of giving a lecture makes you feel shy you should 'pretend' to be more confident. Your students will not know that you are only pretending and it will put them at their ease if they don't have to worry about you.

> I realize what I do: I borrow bits of other people. I really admire Sarah; I love the way she presents. She looks relaxed and confident and calm. I try and pinch a bit of that, try to be a bit more like that.
>
> (A nurse practitioner)

Experienced lecturers often comment on the 'larger than life' versions of themselves that give the big lectures. Actions need to be larger; the voice needs to be projected with greater clarity; pointing to visual aids can be done with the big gesture, etc. Some even feel that there is a certain amount of performance involved and a degree of acting. Pretending to be that eloquent and confident lecturer is a small part of this.

IMMEDIATELY BEFORE THE LECTURE

The half hour before the lecture starts is likely to be the most stressful for a new teacher. Some lecturers like to shut themselves away in a quiet space to think through their notes calmly. Others like to keep themselves busy and occupied right up to the start time. What works best for you?

DON'T FORGET TO BREATHE

For 99.9 per cent of our life we don't think about the act of taking one breath after another and suddenly it becomes a problematic activity. When nervous many speakers take shorter, gasping breaths and, when beginning to speak, may attempt to produce sentences that are far too long, causing them to run out of breath halfway through.

Close your eyes and put your hand on your stomach and simply think about breathing in and out slowly and satisfyingly deeply; breathe in through your nose and out through your nose and mouth. This can be a very calming technique.

Table 3.2 gives some tips on how to breathe properly when presenting and is taken from guidance to students at the University of Pennsylvania.

TABLE 3.2 Guidance from the University of Pennsylvania on correct breathing technique

Breathing correctly when presenting

- Your voice rests on your breath. Inhale before you begin to speak and support your words with your breath as you exhale. (When you are at rest, you inhale and exhale for roughly the same amount of time. When you speak you inhale quickly and exhale slowly).
- Inhale between sentences and phrases and don't wait until you are completely out of breath to inhale.
- Your breathing may slow or increase due to nervousness. These changes can physiologically exacerbate feelings of anxiety. If you notice that you are nervous, dizzy or your thinking is cloudy, take several deep breaths. Make sure that you continue to breathe at an appropriate rate.
- Develop awareness of tension in your throat, chest and stomach. Tension interferes with your breathing and your voice.
- Increase the volume of your voice by increasing the amount of breath that supports your voice.

http://www.sas.upenn.edu/cwic/resources.html

RELAXATION TECHNIQUES

Tension seems to collect in hot spots around the body and the shoulders and neck region seem to be particularly affected. Simply hunching your shoulders up and gently tensing the muscles and then pulling them downwards, breathing out and relaxing them, can really help calm you if you are anxious.

A second area of the body that also obviously shows the symptoms of nerves is the knees which tend to 'lock out' and hold the lecturer's body stiffly and awkwardly when the body is tense. When beginning to present it is helpful to check your knees and 'soften' them by relaxing them and letting them bend very slightly. The body can then find a more relaxed posture and natural balance.

It is also important to relax your voice. You can loosen up your vocal cords by humming up and down the musical scale or going through vocal sounds: A,E,I,O,U.

PROGRESSIVE (MUSCLE) RELAXATION

Dr Edmund Jacobson first described a technique of deep muscle relaxation in 1929. The method involves focusing on different muscle groups,

FIGURE 3.1 Keeping control of the shakes and jitters

contracting them and then consciously letting them relax. Start by squeezing your toes and feet for a count of about ten, then relaxing them. Repeat the squeeze and relax sequence in your lower leg and then continue to work up your body, going slowly and moving from one body part to the next. As you let go of tension in each muscle group, continue to relax the muscles that you've already relaxed so that you can feel the wave of relaxation rising in your body. This full body approach to relaxation is often used at the end of a workout or yoga session too. (See Chapter 5 for further discussion about using and protecting your voice.)

THE FIRST FIVE MINUTES

The very beginning of the lecture is the most difficult for the teacher. Getting going can be hard but once you have found your voice and rhythm you will forget your nerves very quickly. To help get over this initial hump you might find some of the following useful.

Surviving the first few minutes

- Say something inconsequential to begin with just to hear how your voice sounds in the room and to check it is working properly (e.g. 'Good morning. Can you hear me OK up at the back?')
- Show a visual aid early in your lecture; the students will look at it rather than at you which will help you to feel less exposed.
- Find three or four students with friendly faces across the audience who will smile at you and encourage you to keep eye contact with them.
- Avoid holding notes or pointers that exaggerate wobbles and shakes.
- If your knees or legs tremble, lean on the lectern or table. It can also help to shift your weight from one foot to the other or walk around a little.

New lecturers also note when viewing themselves presenting, on video, that they don't look half as nervous as they felt when giving the talk. Nerves always feel worse on the inside. The vast majority of speakers find their 'presenting stride' quickly and never look back through the lecture. Very rarely, very rarely indeed, lecturers will lose their place and forget what is to be said next. This may happen if something has distracted them, e.g. a student has arrived late, or asked a question, or a mobile phone has rung. To prepare for this happening can be reassuring to the nervous presenter, as the fear of mind blanking is much more common than the reality.

FINDING YOURSELF IF YOUR MIND GOES BLANK

The key here is to have your lecture notes in a format that is easy to navigate and move through. People new to lecturing often want to have full lecture notes and some even like to work from a script of sorts. However, once the lecture has begun, the speaker may glance at these notes only rarely, feeling happy that they exist but not really needing to refer to them. So if the lecturer's mind does go blank it is likely that the notes will be out of order with the run of the lecture. It is therefore important to be able to move quickly through the notes and find yourself again speedily. Using small index cards with key words marked in different colours and numbering visual aids may help. Using the notes section of the PowerPoint package to hide speaking notes can also provide this support.

If you prefer to move around the room and write comments on the flipchart or whiteboard it can be useful to hide notes around the teaching 'stage' area so that you know there are backups if you lose your thread.

In one class I write up a list of the stages in a pathway and explain each stage as I go. So I don't forget any, or get them in the wrong order, I make a note of the first letter of each stage on the, folded over, back page of the flipchart. Only I can see them when I stand up to write. I have always remembered them but it puts my mind at ease just to know they are there.

(Demonstrator in biochemistry)

IT DOES GET EASIER

The more you do it the easier it gets and while a small dose of adrenaline is likely to improve your ability to give a good lecture, debilitating anxieties do not. So it is good advice to encourage new teachers actively to seek out opportunities to give lectures and presentations and build up their confidence through experience. After all, it is experiences outside the norm which usually cause stress and not familiar situations. (See Chapter 10 for further guidance on how to learn from your lecture evaluations to improve and develop your skills.)

ISSUES OF CONTROL AND DISCIPLINE

Many teachers never encounter disruptive, rude or aggressive students throughout their teaching career. However, occasionally an individual or a particular class of students can challenge a lecturer through their behaviour and actions. The most common minor difficulties are to do with students arriving late and disrupting the class, mobile phones ringing in the middle of the lecture and students gossiping and texting each other on the back row. These behaviours can be irritating and off-putting and it is worth nipping this rudeness in the bud. How this is

FIGURE 3.2 The different ‘faces’ of disruption

done will depend very much on the teacher's confidence and personality. For example:

Teacher A: confronts the situation head-on and directly
'I do not like mobile phones going off in my lecture. Please make sure you have turned yours off now. You will be asked to leave if it rings in my class'.

Teacher B: appeals for the students' understanding and empathy
'I find mobile phones going off in the lecture very off-putting and I often lose my train of thought. Remember how you feel when you are giving your seminar presentations and please turn your phones off now'.

Teacher C: uses the groundswell of class opinion
'Last week our lecture was disrupted by two mobile phones going off in class and I had a number of students complain to me about this. Please respect your colleagues' rights to study in my class and make sure that you have turned your phones off'.

Teacher D: uses humour to defuse a tense situation when a student actually answers a phone call in the lecture
'Hey can I have a word . . . Oh hello John's mum, very sorry but John is in my lecture at the moment and he is a bit busy. Can he call you back later? Thanks. Bye! OK everybody – let's make sure that doesn't happen again, shall we? You never know who I may end up talking to.'

It is generally best to avoid confrontation in the lecture theatre and certainly important not to lose your temper and professionalism. The spectacle of a furious lecturer embarrassing or fiercely reprimanding a student will not win respect (and could even see the lecturer headlining, unflatteringly, in the unofficial student magazine!).

Lecturers gain and keep control in a lecture through a variety of means:

- their reputation for effort, interest, and enthusiasm for teaching
- their reputation for fairness
- their knowledge of the topic, the equipment and the course

- focusing on the given learning outcomes and what the students need to learn
- responding promptly and fairly to challenges to their authority.

Remember reputations may take a little while to build but can be shattered in minutes.

Students arriving late can cause a stuttering and unsatisfying start to a lecture and some lecturers can feel that the interruptions exacerbate their nerves at the beginning of the lecture. Many colleges and departments have policy statements that provide a supported framework within which you can act, particularly if you wish to consider barring entry to your lecture more than, say, fifteen minutes after the starting time. New/part-time teachers need to make sure that their actions sit comfortably with the departmental view on latecomers and their firm actions would be supported if, for example, students complained about it at a staff/student consultative committee. It is much easier for individual lecturers to enforce a firm policy on late arrivals if all their colleagues enforce it too and the students hear a consistent rule.

It is also a good idea to find out from the students why they are turning up late for your class. It may be out of their control, e.g. the professor in the class before always overruns or their previous class is at the opposite side of the university and they have to dash to yours in five minutes. Berating these students for lateness would be very unfair and a different approach is needed, e.g. consult with the late running professor, talk to the person responsible for timetabling or room booking to make changes, etc.

It is part of your job as a lecturer to maintain an environment in which your students can learn and if a small group of students are chattering or being disruptive the majority of students in the class will be looking to you to take control. Failing to do so will result in a loss of credibility and lead to further discipline problems. It won't go away if you ignore it. Many of the situations that might lead to a chattering group of students being a problem can be avoided. For example, encourage the arriving students to fill up the lecture theatre from the front.

> For my large lecture I make a point of arriving early and standing about halfway up the steep tiered steps. As the students drift in I say good morning and I ask them to sit in front of me, not right at the back.
>
> (Postgraduate Certificate in Education tutor)

I gave my first lectures in a huge lecture theatre, which was very daunting. Some students sat right at the back. It felt very uncomfortable. The third week I rather bravely asked them to move forward. They weren't keen to move but I insisted and now I won't start a lecture until the students come forward, closer to the action.

(History tutor)

What a horrible room I had last year. Very long and narrow, a flat room with pillars blocking the view of several students. There were 120 students in the class and a handful were quite rude, talking and sauntering in late. They always sat at the back of the class and I think they thought that I couldn't see them. I knew I had to do something but I wasn't sure what. What I tried, with some success, was I began teaching from the other side of the room. So suddenly my back row people were my front row students. Just being nearer to my potential troublemakers made me feel more in control and confident.

(Nurse practitioner)

If the room allows it, going and standing near students who don't appear to be working hard enough will often be all that is needed to encourage them to concentrate.

Some student frustrations in the lecture may seem to you to be completely justified if there is poor accommodation, overlapping course curricula or a weakly designed course framework. This may happen if you are a part-time teacher on a course which has been designed and organized by another (more senior) staff member. You may need to anticipate student irritation and questions, and acknowledge real difficulties; you may need to report back to those who can change things, and you may need to explain the situation ('I'm really sorry, we were originally booked into the large lecture theatre but the lights have fused so we are having to make the best of a difficult situation this week – I thank you for your patience'). However, maintain your professional approach and do not undermine your colleagues in front of the students.

Some student behaviour may seem odd and unusual. Remember this may be the result of an emotional or medical disorder. In some cases they may have a registered disability. For example:

I had not been teaching for very long when I was asked to take a few first-year lectures. The group was big and I was nervous. The

> first lecture seemed to go reasonably well with no major hiccups, but as the students were leaving and I was tidying up my notes, I realized one student was actually asleep on the second row. She was roused and left the class – I felt very humiliated that my lecture had been so dull. It was only later when I was talking about it to a colleague that she said 'Oh, I wonder if that's the student who has narcolepsy.' I wasn't even sure I knew what narcolepsy was – but I soon found out the basics and spoke to the student's tutor to see if I should be doing anything in particular for this student.

Very, very rarely a student may appear aggressive and/or unstable to such an extent that it causes the lecturer to have concerns about the safety of that student, other students in the class or, indeed, for themselves. In such extreme cases the student should be asked to leave and university security personnel may need to be involved. If there are ever issues which raise health and safety concerns these should take immediate priority.

> Instructors should direct a student who is being disruptive or threatening to themselves or others to leave the class. If the student refuses to leave after being requested to do so, the instructor should summon University Police to remove the student.
>
> (Extract from *The Instructor's Guidelines for Addressing Disruptive Students in the Classroom*, University of California, Santa Cruz)

Such incidents will need to be reported to the department and the university, as the exclusion of a student from class is clearly a very grave step. It is therefore important to document the incident conscientiously and take appropriate local advice.

FURTHER READING

TA Handbook (2002), *Disruptive Students*, Centre for Teaching Effectiveness, University of Delaware http://www.udel.edu/cte/TAbook/disruptive.html

USEFUL WEB SITES

http://www.aabss.org/journal2001/Fish2001.jmm.html Fish, T. A. and Fraser, I. H. (2001) *Exposing the Iceberg of Teaching Anxiety: A Survey of*

Faculty at Three New Brunswick Universities. Electronic Journal of the American Association of Behavioral and Social Sciences (4).

http://www.tedi.uq.edu.au/Teaching/TertiaryToolbox/TeachingAnxiety.html#Strategies The University of Queensland Teaching and Educational Development Institute's *Toolbox for Tertiary Teaching* gives strategies for overcoming anxiety.

http://www.med.stanford.edu/school/Psychiatry/narcolepsy/ Centre for Narcolepsy, Stanford School of Medicine.

Chapter 4

Structuring lectures

INTRODUCTION

Human beings are obsessed with stories: we read novels, we watch movies and TV and we go to the theatre. Some of our earliest memories are of fairy stories, and narratives of myths and legends underpin our religions and civilizations. Most stories have the same structure: a beginning, a middle and an end: 'Once upon a time there was a prince . . . who had an adventure . . . and they all lived happily ever after.' Human beings clearly feel comfortable with narrative structures like this; they resonate with cognitive structures within that enable them to make sense of the world.

A lecture is also a story and therefore should have a narrative structure; it too needs a beginning, middle and end. If it doesn't have these elements it causes confusion, wastes the mental effort of the audience and leads to poor learning.

A simple way to think about structuring a lecture is to use the sequence below:

- Tell them what you're going to tell them
- Tell them
- Tell them what you've just told them

An alternative way to think about the beginning, middle and end of a lecture is to see them in terms of the following sections:

- Context
- Content
- Closure

We will go through each of these in turn and explain the various components and processes that make them up.

CONTEXT

> What you need is a story that starts with an earthquake and works its way up to a climax.
>
> (Sam Goldwyn, US film producer)

The content of a lecture is embedded and underpinned by a context. The context makes connections with other learning and provides a background from which the importance and relevance of the content to come can be supported. (The term 'set' is also used to describe the initial contextualization of learning, implying that a priming or setting-up process is to be engaged in. However, the word 'set' probably has more meanings than any other word in the English language, hence the term 'context' is preferred.) In terms of the constructivist model of teaching (see series website, Brown 2004) the context is saying 'These bricks are going in this section of the wall, because we're building this part of the house'. It contains a number of important elements that will be described below.

Mood

Assuming the students are already in the lecture theatre a lecture essentially begins when the lecturer walks in through the door. Is the lecturer late? Is the lecturer rushing or relaxed? Does the lecturer take a long time setting up his or her notes and equipment? Does he or she appear to know how to use the lights and the audio-visual equipment? At what point does the lecturer acknowledge the existence of the students and make eye contact?

> I like to be in the lecture theatre before the students and I smile and welcome them as they arrive. This feels less daunting than walking into a full house.
>
> (New history lecturer)

All of these things create a mood out of which the rest of the lecture unfolds. The lecturer should influence the mood and try to make sure it is a positive one. Therefore he or she should not be late, should already know how to use the equipment and should begin by gaining attention (see below), greeting the students in an appropriate way and making eye contact with them. If this is the first time the lecturer has met the students a brief personal introduction should be made. Remember, by not creating a positive mood a negative mood can be created *by default*. Also the opening of the lecture should not be used to apologize for a lack of preparation time or for the amount of information that must be covered. Don't begin by apologizing!

Gaining attention

Some lecturers feel intimidated by the noise and bustle in a large lecture theatre prior to the beginning of a lecture. Inevitably students are talking, laughing and joking and moving around. Sometimes students will ask the lecturer if they can make announcements. Provided there are not too many and they don't take up too much time it creates a good mood if you agree to this and also goes some way to quietening the students down. Some lecturers think that by merely standing at the lectern or overhead projector they will give a signal to the students to stop talking and settle down. Unless the students know the lecturer and are used to his or her working style this is not necessarily the case. Therefore the lecturer should take control. There should be a definite, firm and clear announcement that attention is required and the lecture is about to start. This may be repeated if necessary, increasing the firmness and the volume. Once attention has been gained, greetings and personal introductions, if needed, can be made and the lecture can begin.

Introducing the topic

It is mandatory to introduce the title or the topic of the lecture. 'Thank you for your attention. The subject of today's lecture is . . . X, Y and Z . . .'. The title of the lecture might simultaneously appear on a slide or overhead. At this point it is always worthwhile thinking how you can start with something that will grab the students' attention. It could be a dramatic image that represents a key feature of the lecture; it might be an amusing cartoon; it could involve reading a short piece of poetry or a quotation; it could involve displaying an object or demonstrating an unusual physical phenomenon. A chemist might literally begin with a bang but it is up to the imagination of each lecturer to try to think of something that will make the students sit up and pay attention.

Activating prior learning

The constructivist model of learning (see series website guide, Brown 2004) implies that learning builds upon existing understanding and that new knowledge must be connected to old.

> The most important single factor influencing learning is what the learner already knows. Ascertain this and teach accordingly.
>
> (Ausubel 1968)

Hence it is important during the contextual phase of lecturing to spend a few minutes reviewing and making connections to previous work in a process known as 'activating prior learning'. This is a way of bringing up relevant previous knowledge from memory and placing it, as it were, on the student's mental desktop. This can be done by briefly recalling work done in the previous lecture or lectures, or knowledge that was acquired in the previous year or even at school. If appropriate and feasible it may be done by asking a series of questions that get students to recall previous knowledge.

Once prior learning has been activated connections can start to be made to the newly introduced topic. The lecturer can tell the students that in order to understand the new topic they will need to recall and use their previous knowledge. The amount of activation and the degree to which old material needs to be reviewed is a judgement that the lecturer must make.

Relevance and importance

Explaining the relevance of a new topic will also help connect it to the learners' existing mental framework. The lecturer should be able to make a strong justification for the inclusion of the chosen topic in the curriculum. Communicating the relevance and importance of the topic to the students will help to activate their attention. Relevance means relevant to the overall curriculum outcomes, relevant to future careers and practice, relevant in terms of the intellectual insight and understanding of the topic.

Motivation

The motivation to learn is a complex psychological state influenced by many factors (see series website guide, Brown 2004). It is related to relevance and importance but also has its own dynamic. If the lecturer states that the topic is a core concept that underpins a major area of the course and that it is likely to be assessed, then students are more likely to pay attention. If the topic is concerned with an issue of practice that is very common in future employment again the students might be more motivated to pay attention. Students can also be motivated by the enthusiasm of the lecturer for his or her subject and this is an important attribute of good lecturing practice.

Outlining the structure: signposting

At this point in the context the lecturer should outline the overall structure of the lecture. Different types of lecturing structure will be discussed later but it is useful if the students know what to expect as it provides a cognitive road map for what is to come.

Learning outcomes

Once the topic has been introduced, prior learning activated, students motivated by explaining the relevance and importance of what is to come and the lecture structure outlined, then the lecturer should tell the students what the learning outcomes of the session are going to be. These are statements of what the student should be able to do at the end of the lecture and are essentially the 'added value' in terms of learning that the lecturer has provided. They are normally stated using active verbs such as list, state, describe, apply, and evaluate (see Table 1.2) (see series website guide, Brown 2004). Sessional learning outcomes are the building blocks or scaffolding of the curriculum and should be embedded within the overall course outcomes.

It is important that the outcomes are achievable during the session. For example, to say that one of the learning outcomes is that the student should be able to understand the causes of the First World War is dishonest. Even the professor of history doesn't understand *all* the causes of the First World War; maybe no one fully understands them. What is legitimate is that at the end of the session the student might be able to describe or evaluate some of the common explanations that have been put forward on the causes of the First World War.

A generic context

Can I have your attention please? I'd like to start now.

Thank you. Well, good morning everyone; I'm Dr Jones. It's very nice to meet you all today and I'm going to be taking you for the next few lectures in this module.

Today we're going to be talking about Health and Safety and here's a picture of a man in hospital with an industrial injury which you will see could have been avoided by following straightforward guidance. Now, in order to understand Health and Safety you need to understand the previous work you have done with Dr Smith on hazards in the workplace. Here is a picture of a 'Hazard' just to remind you; this is a diagram of how the hazard assessment process worked and this is how we obtained the final formula for estimating risk of injury.

Well, the concept of safety is a particularly important core concept. If you understand safety you will be able to make sense of governance and legislation issues later in the course. Also, first aid is very useful and if any of you get jobs dealing with industrial injuries you will be using a knowledge of first aid principles almost all the time. The incidence of stress is so high that it has major resource implications.

What I'm going to do in this lecture is firstly talk about how workplace hazards lead directly into Health and Safety. Then I'm going to give you an overview of the underlying concepts in Health and Safety. Then I'm going to show you a few examples of how a knowledge of Health and Safety can help you solve common problems in this area and then finally we'll have a look at a case study to show you how you can evaluate its effectiveness in practice.

At the end of this session you should be able to explain how an analysis of workplace hazards leads directly to Health and Safety, list and describe the main features of Health and Safety, use Health and Safety to solve some common problems and evaluate the effectiveness of Health and Safety in practice. Clearly these will be the type of things we'll be sampling from you in the end of module exam.

CONTENT

If the context has been adequately dealt with the students should be primed and ready to deal with the substantive content of the lecture. The content of a lecture can be 'life, the universe and everything', but there are some generic principles that, if adhered to, ensure that the lecture is effective. These are listed below and then explained in more detail.

- Control the amount of content.
- Vary the stimulus.
- Structure the content.
- Navigate your structure.
- Use well thought-out explanations.
- Stimulate thinking.

Control the amount of content

One of the commonest errors that lecturers make is trying to present too much material. Slide after slide, overhead after overhead, example after example the information pours out of the lecturer and the students end up trying to drink from a fire hose. As discussed earlier, a lecture should be an overview of a key area given by an expert who can explain core concepts and who is aware of the difficulties and pitfalls in understanding. A lecture should not be used to convey large quantities of information that can be read in textbooks or given in handouts.

One of the reasons that lecturers present too much information is the erroneous belief that if they 'cover' an area of knowledge in a lecture the students will automatically learn it. This is simply not true. Learning comes from engaging with the material in a stimulating way, not trying to memorize reams of facts passively.

So how can a lecturer decide how much material to present in a lecture? Clearly the lecturer should liaise with the coordinator for the module or course in question to ensure that the overall distribution of content between the lectures has been distributed equitably. It should also be kept in mind that content can be learned via other means such as self-directed learning, e.g. reading. With this in mind the lecturer should attempt to minimize the amount of detail in the lecture and concentrate on core facts, concepts and explanations. Detail and further examples should be relegated to further reading.

A useful slogan in dealing with the amount of content is:

Less is more

Paradoxically the less the lecturer teaches, the more the students will understand and remember. The more the lecturer teaches, the less they will understand.

Vary the stimulus

One of the other major problems of lecturing is the boring, monotonous presentation that sends the audience to sleep. It is known that people's attention span in lectures dips after about fifteen to twenty minutes (Johnstone and Parcival 1976) and that, particularly after lunch, if the lights are dim, a significant number of people in the audience will struggle to keep awake. The average lecture slot is one hour, the lecture itself being slightly shorter allowing for students to enter and leave the lecture theatre. Students will quite happily watch a film or play for two hours or more without falling asleep so it is not merely the length of time that causes the problem. The problem is caused by exposure to a constant unchanging stimulus: the lecturer's monotonous, unmodulated voice; the regular display of slides or overheads that all look the same; the unstimulating presentation of information; the absence of any other presentation modality. What keeps an audience awake during a two-hour film or play are constant variations of stimulation. Writers and directors know that, just as with a symphony, a narrative that is going to grab attention has to contain fast and slow movements; it has to have drama and excitement; it has to have changes of pace. Ensuring that no one presentation method is used for more than ten to fifteen minutes without a change is a good idea.

Humour is also a wonderful mechanism for not only varying the stimulus but also helping people remember things. Lecturers can collect humorous images and cartoons that help illustrate particular points and intersperse them throughout the lecture. However, be careful! Humour to one person might be offensive to another. Be sensitive to the gender, cultural and religious differences within the student audience when using humour.

See Chapter 6 for further discussion of student activity and interactivity in lectures.

Structure the content

Students in general do not want to go on a 'magical mystery tour' during a lecture. They don't want to be taken on a random walk through disconnected concepts and facts; they want to be able to see the relationships between ideas. The only way this can be achieved is by means of a logical and reasoned structure which acts as a framework for the main content of the lecture.

Brown and Atkins (1988) list a number of ways a lecture or presentation can be structured: the 'classical', the 'sequential', the 'problem-centred' and the 'comparative'. These, and further examples of structure, are outlined below.

Classical: 1, 1.1, 1.2, 1.3, 2, 2.1, 2.2, 2.3 . . .

This, commonly used, type of structure might be found when the lecture is concerned with listing a series of related entities and describing their features or properties. For example, it might be a series of diseases with their symptoms, investigations and treatments; a series of organisms with their anatomical features; a series of political leaders with their backgrounds, policies and achievements. The overall structure might concern itself with comparing and contrasting the various entities.

Sequential: a then b then c then d . . .

This is possibly the commonest type of lecturing structure, in which the lecturer goes through a simple sequence of related sub-topics that underpin the main topic and form a logical and coherent 'narrative' with a specific conclusion. Care needs to be taken to ensure students are understanding each progressive step.

Process: a then b then c then d then a

There are cyclical processes to be described in biochemistry, ecology, geology, economics and many other disciplines. Using the sequence of components within the process itself will provide a logical and coherent lecturing framework.

Chronological

Clearly temporal and historical sequences provide a ready-made framework for structuring lectures. History itself or the development of a scientific or technological theory or process can be structured in this way.

Spatial

The spatial relationships between entities is a useful teaching framework. Anatomy and embryology can be taught in this way but other subjects involving spatial relationships such as geography, architecture or engineering can benefit from this approach. For example, in anatomy the three-dimensional structure of a limb could be described in a sequence that might build up from the skeleton, then muscles, then blood supply and nerves and finally the layers of skin and subcutaneous fat. In geography a country might be described in terms of its major cities, rivers and mountains and the relationships between them. In architecture the design of a medieval cathedral might be described in terms of the spatial relationships between its major structural features such as apse, nave and arches.

Comparative: pros and cons, advocacy and controversy

Some very stimulating learning can be generated by setting up a debate between competing ideologies, concepts, methods, procedures or techniques. The lecturer can give the case or evidence for one and then shift to the other side. This is an ideal situation for student involvement and students might be asked to contribute to the debate or vote at the end. If another lecturer is available then the two sides of the argument can be delivered by two different people, turning it into a genuine debate. The technique can also be used for other dichotomous entities such as comparing the normal with the abnormal in medicine.

Induction and deduction

The process by which observations, facts and evidence are synthesized together to form theories, rules and laws is known as induction. The opposite process by which theories and rules are used to predict and calculate facts about the world is known as deduction. Both processes generate inductive and deductive reasoning and can be used as the basis for structuring lectures. For example, an inductive teaching structure can be used to show how facts and evidence eventually led to the development of a theoretical framework. On the other hand, a lecture might begin with the exposition of a theory and then show how it can be used to deduce or predict specific facts about the world. The implications of these two forms of reasoning in developing explanations will be discussed below.

Problems and case studies

Inductive and deductive reasoning are brought together in the hypothetico-deductive system that characterizes scientific, technical and clinical diagnostic reasoning used in problem solving. Problems and case studies are an ideal vehicle for structuring teaching episodes as they bring together conceptual understanding and reasoning with real-life, relevant situations. For example, a clinician absorbs the symptoms and signs of illness during history taking and examination and, by means of induction, comes up with hypotheses about what the problem might be in the form of a set of differential diagnoses. In order to test the validity of the diagnoses and to differentiate between them, further examinations and investigations are carried out based on possible deductions from the hypotheses. On the basis of the results some hypotheses are eliminated, and so on, until a final diagnosis is arrived at. The same process is carried out by a car mechanic or electronic technician in attempting to diagnose a fault.

Lectures structured around problems and case studies might come at the end of a series of more conceptually orientated lectures but they provide a valuable opportunity to synthesize and summarize many key ideas while emphasizing important reasoning processes.

Navigate your structure

Having a teaching structure is all very well for the lecturer but it should also be communicated to the audience to help them navigate their way through the narrative. To a certain extent this process should have begun during the context phase when the lecturer briefly went through the overall structure of the session. However, once into the content it is helpful to inform the students where they have been, where they are and what they should be looking at, and where they are going. This is very much like the process that occurs in a good textbook where, in addition to headings and subheadings, the author talks directly to the reader indicating, for example, that a topic has now been finished, that a new topic is to be discussed, that an important definition is being outlined or that it is now time to summarize. The terms signposts, frames, foci and links have been used to describe these navigational markers, which are discussed below (Brown and Atkins 1988).

Signposts

These are statements that signal the direction you are going to take.

> Well, what I'm going to do in this lecture is firstly talk about how hazard analysis leads directly into Health and Safety issues. Then I'm

> going to give you an overview of the underlying concepts in Health and Safety. Then I'm going to show you a few examples of how a knowledge of Health and Safety can help you solve common problems in this area and then finally we'll have a look at a case study to show you how you can evaluate its effectiveness in practice.

Frames

These are statements indicating the beginning and ends of topics and sections.

> We've now explained how hazard analysis leads on to Health and Safety so let's now look at Health and Safety in more detail.

Foci

These are statements that highlight and emphasize key ideas, definitions and concepts.

> What you're looking at there is one of the most important definitions in this particular area, so pay particular attention to it.

Links

These are statements connecting to other sections of the lecture or to prior knowledge and experience.

> So now you can see how Health and Safety builds on the ideas in hazard analysis and also relates to earlier concepts you might have come across in Module X last year.

Use well thought-out explanations

If, as discussed earlier, a lecture is an overview of a key area given by an expert who can explain core concepts and who is aware of the difficulties and pitfalls in understanding, then explaining is one of the most important teaching and lecturing techniques and structures. This is where the lecturer can give understanding by making connections between concepts and facts. It is also about ensuring that misunderstandings do not arise and a good lecturer should be aware of common misunderstandings and how they can be avoided.

A common error that novice lecturers make is assuming that because they understand something they can explain it to another without thinking about how they are going to do it beforehand. They may prepare a lecture, including some concepts or processes that need to be explained which they, as experts, are familiar with, only to discover that in the act of explaining they trip over themselves and make a mess of it. The key idea to remember is that just because you understand something doesn't mean you can explain it to someone else. The opposite side to this, as many lecturers will testify, is that you don't *really* understand something until you *can* explain it to someone else.

Therefore explanations need to be thought through in the preparation phase of lecturing (see Chapter 2). From the constructivist model of learning we can deduce that new knowledge must connect to old to help build up understanding. Lecturers must know 'where the students are at' or what knowledge they already have, and must activate this prior knowledge. They must then use a variety of techniques, which will shortly be described, to make bridges from this knowledge to the new knowledge they wish the students to know. This mental 'scaffolding' was termed the 'zone of proximal development' by the Russian psychologist Vygotsky (1978).

So what are the techniques that can be used to build bridges to new understanding? Learners can only use the knowledge they already have to build new knowledge from the experiences they are having. Therefore the teacher must start with this knowledge and make use of it. If a new concept is the logical outcome of combining existing concepts, facts or evidence then the lecturer needs to ensure there is a seamless set of connections from the old to the new with no gaps or mental jumps that some students might not grasp. Brown and Atkins (1988) suggest that such explanations should follow a sequence analogous to the proof of a geometrical theorem which seamlessly starts from a set of axioms and leads on logically to its conclusion.

However, sometimes a concept is so new or unusual that additional help is required. This is where analogy, metaphor and the use of concrete imagery to represent abstract concepts should be used when constructing explanations. By using and extending existing cognitive structures the lecturer can create a 'pre-conceptual' model from which the learner can relatively easily jump to the final concept. When constructing explanations there is some evidence that people find inductive reasoning easier than deductive reasoning. Both Piaget (1969) and Bruner (1968) looked at the development of 'concrete' and 'abstract' reasoning and suggested that concrete reasoning, thinking about facts and entities in the real world, precedes and is easier than abstract or highly logical reasoning, which is the highest form of human cognition. Bruner further argued that although adults are characterized by their ability to use abstract reasoning they frequently flip back down to concrete reasoning when thinking gets tough. One only needs to recall asking for a 'concrete example', when trying to understand an abstract concept, to appreciate how much easier it is for us to conceptualize and manipulate real entities in our mind's eye than abstract ones. If this is the case it further reinforces the idea that explanations of complex abstract ideas should use concrete examples where possible. Lecturers should be sensitive to the fact that within any given group of students there will be a range of abilities in relation to the ease with which they can move from the concrete to the abstract.

There are other individual differences, which influence the ability to deal with particular explanations, that might be found within a student audience. It is well established that students have different learning styles, see page 7 (Honey and Mumford 1982) and will be more or less attracted to different ways of learning. In addition it is further suggested that individuals are more or less dominated by their right brain or left brain. According to studies of brain localization (Springer and Deutsch 1993), the left-hand side of the brain is where logical and linguistic information is processed whereas the right-hand side of the brain is concerned with imagery and holism. Furthermore, Gardner has suggested that we have six independent intelligences: linguistic, logico-mathematical, spatial, musical, kinaesthetic and personal, and that once again individuals are more or less dominated by particular modalities (Gardner 1993).

This implies that lecturers should use a variety of audio-visual and computer-assisted aids to create illustrations which might appeal to individual cognitive differences in the student audience. Using PowerPoint it is relatively easy to create attractive animated diagrams and it is also possible to display computer simulations or digitized video through a data projector to a large audience. Such images and animations, when interspersed with text and an oral presentation, make a multi-media presentation that is highly likely to have strong explanatory power to just about everyone in the audience.

Stimulate thinking

The whole process of structuring, organizing and developing explanatory sequences in a lecture should aim to interest and stimulate the audience; to make them think. Without that the lecture will be merely a boring recital of facts that the students will attempt to record without any intellectual engagement. We have already discussed the structures that can be used to organize a lecture and to a large extent these should encourage thinking by the way they relate the material together into a coherent sequence. The use of appropriate explanations should also encourage thinking. However, there are many different types of thinking and the aim should be to encourage the highest level of thinking possible. Below is a list of some common thinking categories that lecturers should be aware of when planning and organizing lectures. At any point in the lecture what type of thinking are the students engaged in?

- analysing
- synthesizing
- logical reasoning
- hypothetic-deductive reasoning
- evaluating evidence or data
- appraising and judging
- critical evaluation
- applying knowledge to new contexts
- seeing new relationships
- creative speculation
- lateral thinking
- designing
- problem solving.

Finishing the content

Before I summarize are there any questions?

As the lecturer moves towards the end of the content phase of the lecture there should be a sense of reaching a conclusion in the narrative process. The main arguments and explanations should have been put forward and the students should have been able to achieve the learning outcomes set out in the context phase. However, there may still be some students who haven't understood every single point or have been stimulated to think of some questions.

The tradition has been to summarize the lecture and then ask: 'Are there any questions?' However, experience shows that once students see that the lecture is being summarized they mentally disengage and will start to pack away their pens and notepads. The majority of students now want to leave the lecture theatre and the last thing on their mind is to ask questions. Therefore it is appropriate that at this point the lecturer states:

> Before I summarize the key points of this lecture there are a few minutes left for you to ask any questions you might have. If there's anything you haven't quite understood or if there's anything that you'd like an answer to, put up your hand and I'll be pleased to try and answer.

Students might also be encouraged to go through their notes looking for gaps or missing information. One technique is to ask the students to note down individual lecture summaries for themselves before the lecturer recaps. This activity not only encourages students to participate in the process, but it can also provide the teacher with some feedback on how well the students have understood. *Final questioning should be seen as part of the content.*

(Of course, depending on the nature of the lecture and the lecturer, questioning might already have been a feature of the proceedings. Here we are assuming a 'conventional' lecture where questions are left, more or less, to the end. We will discuss the method of 'active lecturing' in Chapter 6.)

The lecturer may also want to give additional information to the students at the end of a session. See Table 4.1 for some suggestions.

CLOSURE

> And they all lived happily ever after.

As discussed above, the end of the content should include the conclusions reached and the 'take-home' messages. The closure phase should summarize the key points that arose during the presentation. A useful way of doing this is to show the learning outcomes that were the focus of the lecture. Going through each one and emphasizing that they have

TABLE 4.1 Final remarks – points a lecturer may wish to make at the end of the session

And finally . . .

- Sources of further information and additional reading.
- How to contact the lecturer with queries.
- Acknowledgements.
- Links to VLEs or web-based course support mechanisms, e.g. 'You can find the full reading list on Blackboard and ten quick self-test questions so that you can check your own understanding.'
- Reminders of work deadlines or course assessment requirements.
- Links to support tutorials or practical/laboratory sessions', e.g. 'Today we have looked at the theory. Tomorrow morning you will have the chance to experiment with the variables in the lab.'
- Thank the students for attending, e.g. 'Thanks very much for working hard today. Have a good weekend and I will see you back here for part two next week.'

been achieved is an easy way to summarize. Then any conclusions reached can be mentioned yet again for emphasis. However, it is also helpful during the summary of the outcomes to revisit some of the motivational ideas mentioned during the context phase. Now that the students have achieved the outcomes they should leave the lecture theatre with a sense of achievement and feeling confident that they can now do the things promised earlier. Furthermore, they should now be motivated to engage in independent study.

EXAMPLES FROM DIFFERENT DISCIPLINES

General practice

Whenever I plan a session now I always start by thinking what learning outcomes I want the students to achieve. Once I've nailed that I work backwards and everything else usually falls into place.

(General practice lecturer)

Nursing

I've gradually realized the importance of explaining the relevance and importance of what I'm lecturing on at the beginning. I normally make presentations to ten or twenty people at a time so the group is small enough for some interactivity, even though it's really a lecture. But I do notice how people pay more attention and seem to be more interested if I've explained how they'll be able to use the knowledge I'm imparting.

(Nurse practitioner lecturer)

Biochemistry

We all have to give the students learning objectives (outcomes) now for each session and they go up on the Networked Learning Environment and form part of the curriculum map. At first I thought it was just more work and imposing meaningless educational ideas on us. But over the years I've realized that having them really does clarify my teaching and focus what I do and I've changed them around quite a bit and made sure they fit with the assessment system. However, it sometimes worries me that that's all the students will learn now, just the learning objectives. I'd like them to read around the subject more and do more than just the bottom line but I suppose I'm old fashioned. We never had learning objectives when I was at university; we used to work out what to learn by using past examination papers.

(Biochemistry lecturer)

Chemistry

It's true what they say about not really understanding something until you've taught it. I remember a few years ago when I'd just started lecturing being in an Honours lecture and completely seizing up in the middle of an explanation of this process I was explaining. I'm not sure if the students actually noticed it. I went away afterwards and really looked at it and thought about it until I felt I could explain it. Now I can do that explanation OK. It made me realize that you can get away with bad explanations to students half of the time because they think they can't understand it because they're not clever enough. They never think it's your fault.

(Chemistry lecturer)

FURTHER READING

Brown, G. A. and Atkins, M. (1992) *Effective Teaching in Higher Education*. London: Routledge.

Brown, S. and Race, P. (2002) *Lecturing: A Practical Guide*. London: Kogan Page.

Egan, M. (1997) *Would You Really Rather Die Than Give a Talk?* New York, NY: Amacom.

Race, P. (1999) '2000 tips for lecturers' in *Lectures*. London: Kogan Page.

USEFUL WEB SITES

http://www4.gvsu.edu/ftlc/lectures.htm Robert and Mary Pew Faculty Teaching and Learning Centre.

http://www.irc.uci.edu/trg/56.html The 'Giving Effective Lectures' page gives links to 'Suggestions for Effective Lecture Preparation and Delivery' in the *Teaching Resources Guide* produced by the Instructional Resources Centre at the University of California, Irvine.

Chapter 5

Using your voice effectively and presenting material visually

INTRODUCTION

This chapter is about using the tools of communication and lecturing effectively and starts by looking at how to use the voice well. Often forgotten in a discussion of audio-visual aids, it remains our most valuable communication tool and tutors need to look after their voice, use it properly and consider how to use it to best effect in the lecture. The chapter also looks at how lecturers choose to present themselves in a lecture through their dress code and introductions.

The discussion of audio-visual aids is relatively brief and focuses particularly on the design of material for visual delivery. The use of C&IT and a wider range of teaching resources is the subject of a companion volume in this series by Paul Chin (2004), so please consult this book for further information about equipment and technology etc.

USING YOUR VOICE EFFECTIVELY IN A LECTURE

We talk all the time (some more than others) but lecturing is different. In trying to project our voice and make ourselves understood in a lecture theatre we use the voice quite differently.

The kinds of delivery problems commonly observed in lectures are:

- a monotone and flat delivery which doesn't hold attention and bores the students
- the volume and clarity of intonation dropping off towards the end of sentences

- the failure to use emphasis and pauses to stress important points and punctuate delivery
- regional or national accents that obscure meaning for some students, particularly those from overseas or those who have hearing difficulties
- not facing the students when addressing them
- getting the pace of delivery wrong.

PACE OF DELIVERY

Perhaps the most common problem experienced by many new teachers is getting the speed of delivery wrong, and in many cases that means talking too quickly. This is often associated with nerves and therefore may be much more pronounced at the beginning of the lecture. It may also be associated with having too much to say in the time available and having to speed up towards the end. This is actually a problem to be addressed in preparation. However, some people do slow down and seem to labour points or become very hesitant and apparently 'unsure' in their delivery. Trying to get a good pace and flow to the lecture is clearly important and may take a little time and practice to get right.

> Do you know your own demons? If you don't it is very helpful to video yourself when explaining, or to record your voice while lecturing and then to critically review your oral delivery. Alternatively, ask a colleague to observe one of your lectures and ask them to watch your students' reactions and to give you feedback on pacing.

THE SPOKEN WORD

There are differences between the spontaneous spoken word and reading from a written text. It is easier to listen and understand when the lecturer speaks in shorter sentences in which the subject and the verb are near the beginning of the sentence. Multi-layered sentences with lots of semicolons or 'ands' make it easier for the listener to mishear and misunderstand. Longer and more complex sentences may also be much more difficult for the lecturer to say fluently. Reading from notes, a script or a computer screen also prevents lecturers from keeping a good level of eye contact with the audience and can give the impression that they are 'talking to themselves' rather than communicating with their students.

FORMING WORDS AND SENTENCES

Very simple words can suddenly become tongue-twisters in the mouth of a nervous lecturer and so it is important to think about the language you choose and try to avoid, where possible, the words which you find difficult to pronounce (especially at the beginning of your talk). If difficult words are unavoidable it can be helpful to make a point of pausing before tackling them, and if appropriate make a feature of writing them on the board so that students have the correct spelling. The students will therefore use both the visual and the oral communication to gain understanding and clarity and it helps to take the pressure off the speaker. Using humour may also help here; you can comment that this is a bit of a tongue-twister or invite the students to have a go at saying it too? These are all tactics aimed at reducing the emphasis of 'performance' from the lecturer. How much the lecture feels like a theatrical event will clearly depend on the size of the lecture, the material being presented and the student and staff expectations but it will also depend upon your personal and preferred style of lecturing.

LOOKING AFTER YOUR VOICE

Voice coaches advise that you should lubricate your vocal folds (vocal cords) when you speak, so taking a glass of still water into the lecture theatre with you is important. Before giving a lecture, relax and gently stretch out the muscles around your shoulders and neck to prepare the muscles in your throat. Some teachers may also warm up their vocal folds – a commonly used voice exercise is to run through vowel sounds a few times (A,E,I,O,U), and for each letter exaggerate the pronunciation and movements of the mouth.

When lecturing try to keep your chin and neck at a comfortable and relaxed 90-degree angle to help avoid tension and strain (for the same reasons it is bad for your voice to cradle a telephone under your chin and chat for hours!). To help achieve this find two or three friendly faces in the audience of students and try and move your eye contact around the lecture theatre. Avoid looking down at your notes, or shoes, for too long and try not to crane your neck upwards in very steep lecture theatres.

Avoid raising your voice to get students' attention. If you organize an 'in-class' discussion or buzz group (see Chapter 6) agree with the students, before they begin their conversations, how you will interrupt their discussions ready to resume your lecturing input, e.g. by turning on the overhead projector. The steady pace of your delivery and your clear enunciation will do more to let your students hear and understand you than the increased volume of your speech, i.e. speak more clearly and slowly rather than just more loudly.

WORDS OF ADVICE

Straining your voice to make yourself heard in a full and bustling lecture theatre; talking without a break for one or two hours at a stretch; doing this daily in October after a summer away from the lecture theatre – it is no wonder that many of the voice and throat problems (e.g. laryngitis and nodules on vocal folds) that are taken to doctor's surgeries and hospitals belong to teachers and lecturers.

Learning how to use your voice in a way that is sustainable and effective is vitally important. Here are some quick tips:

In summary

- Keep vocal folds (or vocal cords) well lubricated when speaking: take in a glass of still water to drink which is not too cold.
- Try and keep your neck in a relaxed position when talking. The vocal folds are at their optimal working position when your head and neck are roughly at 90 degrees to each other and your chin is held up a little.
- Don't shout to get attention; speak more clearly and slowly (use turning on the overhead projector or stage lights to get attention). If the room is very large you may need a microphone.
- Avoid drinking alcohol or too much strong coffee and smoking before lecturing.

To learn more about voice problems and how to take care of your voice look at the NIDCD (National Institute of Deafness and Other Communication Disorders) web site which provides further web links and straightforward guidance: (http://www.nidcd.nih.gov/index.asp).

FINDING A PERSONAL STYLE

I always feel as though I have to make everything larger than life. I seem to slightly exaggerate the way I talk and even the way I move and point to things. The bigger the lecture the more I feel like I'm acting.

(New teacher in law)

When reading about teaching and learning and relating it to how you give a lecture it is important to develop your own style. Observing others teaching, thinking about role models and remembering what we found helpful in lectures, as students can help formulate ideas of how we would like to lecture. However, it is important to work to our own strengths and to incorporate techniques and practices that best suit the material, the context and that personal style.

The use of humour has been mentioned in Chapter 4 and some lecturers may comfortably crack jokes or show cartoons to very good effect; others may wish to run their lectures solely around interactive activities such as exercises or open discussions. Some use music to help create a particular atmosphere, to give their students a relaxing break or to emphasize a learning point. Some teachers work exclusively from their visual aids and handout material while others build in greater flexibility and are happy to work more spontaneously in parts of their lecture.

Choosing to ask your students to do a football-style 'Mexican wave' to demonstrate how nerve synapses work may not suit everyone's personal style. You have to find your own, without it curtailing your ability to innovate and experiment occasionally. If you are the kind of person who doesn't often tell jokes, don't choose the moment when you are standing in front of 200 first-year students, on a Monday morning, to try and tell one.

HOW DO YOU CHOOSE TO PRESENT YOURSELF?

Some lecturers feel more confident and comfortable if they adopt a particular dress code when they lecture.

A number of experienced teachers attending a teaching and learning workshop were asked how they dress to lecture:

FIGURE 5.1 Finding your own style

I always put on a jacket; it makes me feel ready and professional.

When I lecture to the Medics I don't wear my jeans. They have to look smart when they work on the wards and in the clinics and I feel I should do the same for them.

Some of my colleagues wear a suit to lecture in, but I want to look more approachable so I tend to go for smart but casual.

When I get nervous I blush down my neck, so I always wear a shirt with a fairly high collar to hide this – it makes me feel a bit more confident.

How teachers choose to introduce themselves is also variable. A formal 'Hello. I am Dr Green from the history department' may be appropriate for a large first-year class. The same teacher may choose to use 'Good morning. I'm Jo and I will be taking your next three lectures' for a smaller final-year class or in an evening lecture with mature students. There are no rules and new teachers may wish to think through the kind of 'first impression' they wish to create.

PRESENTING MATERIAL VISUALLY

Having worked hard to make the most of your oral delivery the strong advice is: don't just rely on it. Use visual stimulation to help your students understand and learn better in your lecture.

There are many ways you can introduce visual stimuli into the classroom. The list below is divided into two groups: first, those visual aids which are generated and produced 'live' in front of the class and second, those which are pre-prepared and then shown during the lecture.

Generated in class

- Visual demonstrations.
- Flipchart pages and instant posters.
- Blackboard and whiteboard notes.
- Interactive whiteboards and panels (see Chapter 8 for further information).

Pre-prepared

- Overhead projection slides (OHPs).
- Computer-aided presentations using packages such as Microsoft PowerPoint (PP).
- Slides (less commonly used these days in many disciplines).
- Posters.
- Video clips.

CHOICE OF AUDIO-VISUAL AIDS

Both Race (1999) and Baume and Baume (1996) stress the educational importance of selecting appropriate visual aids according to purpose. When presenting at a conference you may wish to make a good impression with the audience, look very professional and actually avoid being interrupted by questions during your presentation, in which case choosing to use PowerPoint is very appropriate. Alternatively you may be giving a lecture to thirty students whom you wish to engage in dialogue and discussion during the lecture, and the material you wish to present is basically textual. In this situation, especially if you are working in an unfamiliar teaching room, it may be more appropriate to use an overhead projector. To collect and record the

TABLE 5.1 Reasons to select different visual aids

Overhead projector	PowerPoint presentation	Flipchart
Commonly available	Looks attractive, professional and up-to-date	Can produce a visual aid on the spot
Can face the students when talking	Can easily edit and update your presentation	Can produce a 'live' record of notes in the class
Simple technology, less likely to go wrong	Can incorporate video clips, simulations, graphics etc.	Very low-tech. 'Nothing can go wrong'
Can keep the lights up	Can make handout materials easily	Students can use flipcharts to share their views
Can pre-prepare slides relatively inexpensively (using PowerPoint software?)	Can make the presentation available to students on the web or on CD	Can be used to slow down a 'fast talker' (as can writing on a board)
Can be used repeatedly and updated simply	Storing and transporting presentations on CDs is easy	
Can be flexible in delivery, skip, swap order or repeat slides	Can incorporate hyperlinks to relevant websites	

feedback from students during your class on a flipchart would be a good choice.

To help you decide which equipment and approach would best suit your needs and purposes, Table 5.1 lists some good reasons to use an overhead projector, a projected PowerPoint presentation or a flipchart.

For more on the comparative costs and benefits of OHP transparencies and PowerPoint slide presentations in lectures look at Belinda Ho's paper, *From Using Transparencies to Using PowerPoint slides in the Classroom* (http://www.aare.edu.au/01pap/ho01072.htm).

GENERATING VISUAL AIDS IN THE LECTURE

The white or blackboard, the flipchart, the interactive whiteboard are all examples of visual aid equipment that allow the lecturer, or the students, to produce explanatory aids or a record of events during the class. Teachers in some disciplines make extensive use of this form of equipment, using it to work through explanations or derivations in front of the students in real time. In mathematics, for example, board work has long been a core aspect of many lectures, the teacher explaining steps in a solution as he or she works through problems in front of the students. To do this well there are some pretty obvious pointers.

Using blackboards and whiteboards

- Clean boards fully before you start (and clean them when you finish your class).
- Take care to write big enough and neatly enough for students to be able to read it from the back of the room.
- Plan the use of board space (see Figure 5.2).
- Don't try to talk and write at the same time as you end up talking to the board and not to the students (this can cause great difficulties for students with hearing difficulties who are partially relying on lip-reading or for non-native speakers of English who may use body language and facial expressions to help them gain a full understanding).

The lecturer will clearly have to respond to the nature of the facilities available in the teaching room and work out the most effective way to plan the use of board space. Rollover boards need to be raised up to ensure visibility, particularly in steeply tiered lecture theatres. Long, wide boards can be readily divided into 'pages' and interactive whiteboards can be used to print off or download copies of the board work for students to take away with them.

Using flipcharts

Position the flipchart so that you can use it comfortably. Right-handed people often prefer the flipchart to be on the left so that they only need to turn a little to write on the flipchart and then look back towards the students. Holding the flipchart firmly in the left hand and writing with the right also helps to keep writing neat and even.

a. A continuous explanation on a large horizontal board

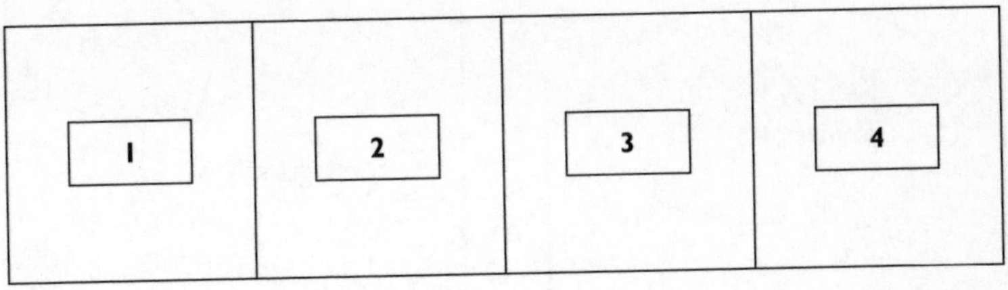

Starting writing in section 1 and moving on to section 2 and so on to section 4. When the board is full return to section 1. And clean and reuse sections in turn. This means that the students will have plenty of time to copy down any notes they may want long before the board needs to be cleaned.

b. Retaining points of reference throughout the lecture

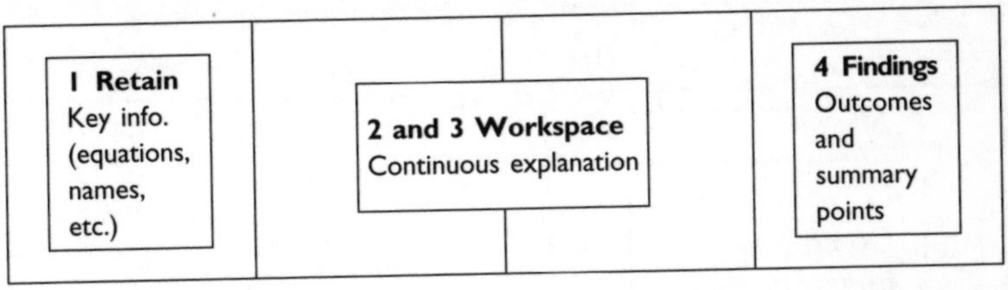

Important information that will be used and referred to throughout the lecture is written up and kept (1). Outcomes or generated findings are collected together as a summary section (4) which is added to during the lecture. The centre of the board is the work area for the class.

c. Two opposing views or explanations – compared and contrasted.

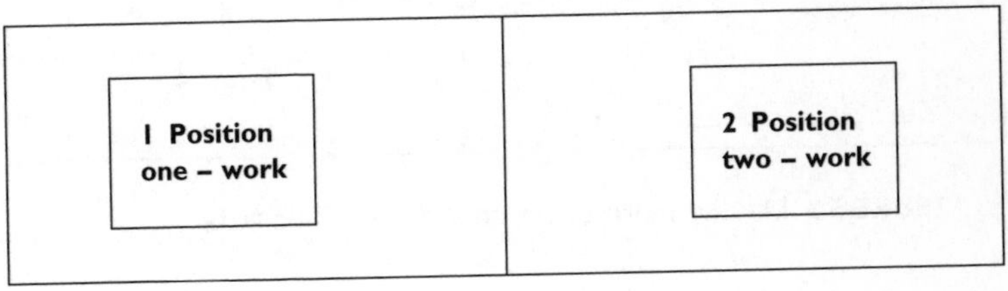

FIGURE 5.2 Planning the use of board space

Just because a visual aid is being produced in the class doesn't mean that it should be messy and untidy. Take care to lay out the page attractively and do not cramp or scribble your writing. Use bullet points and spacing to ensure that everyone can read it. Do not be in too much of a hurry and if you feel too rushed to write properly then

FIGURE 5.3 Making more of an impact with flipcharts

abbreviate or ask a student to act as scribe for you (but remember this student will also want time to note-take or take part in discussions too).

Flipchart art can be used to make your pages more visually appealing or to emphasize learning points. Figure 5.3 shows some simple designs that can be easily incorporated into the flipchart work of the most unartistic new teacher. For more ideas consult Lucas (2000).

Using the interactive whiteboard

An interactive whiteboard is a large, touch-sensitive panel that connects to a digital projector and a computer, displaying the information on the computer screen. It looks like a traditional whiteboard and can be used in the same way. The computer connected to the interactive whiteboard can be controlled by touching the board directly or by using a special pen.

The use of this technology has really taken off in infant and junior schools as it allows very young children, who may have less well developed fine motor skills, to use it. It is also being used extensively in education programmes designed for people with disabilities or learning difficulties. Interactive whiteboards or SMART boards are beginning to be used in higher education although at the time of writing the technology is not widely available in lecture theatres. However, because this technology combines the traditional and the new – the chalkboard and all the resources of a multimedia computer (graphics, video and sound, etc.) – its use as a dynamic presentational tool is likely to expand rapidly.

USING PRE-PREPARED VISUAL AIDS

Using the overhead projector (OHP)

The machine itself

Most obviously, know your equipment. There are lots of different models that have slightly different controls for focusing and altering the intensity of projected light. Moving the OHP when it is switched on can blow the bulb. Many OHPs contain a spare bulb and you can quickly switch from one to another by turning it off, lifting up the glass top and swivelling the second bulb across into position. Some older styles of machine don't have this facility, so either have a spare OHP or have a contingency plan. If you do blow a bulb don't forget to report it to audio-visual services.

Setting up

Try to tilt the screen so that the sides of the image are parallel to the sides of the screen and the image is centred and even. This is known as the keystone. Organize the furniture and your own position so that the students can see the screen and you are not standing in front of the screen or getting in the way as you point to the slide.

Preferences

It is probably better to put an acetate slide onto the OHP while it is switched off so that the transparency is perfectly positioned when it's illuminated. However, switching the machine on and off between several slides can be very irritating. If you are not referring to the slides turn the machine off – the projector's cooling fans are often noisy.

'Revelation' divides audience opinion; some people like it and some hate it. This practice involves placing a piece of paper across or under the acetate slide so that selected parts of the image are kept hidden from the viewers until you are ready for them to see it. It can help to focus the students' attention on the relevant points as you talk about them and it can help lecturers to pace themselves. However, some students will find the concealment distracting and irritating, wondering more about what you are hiding from them than what you are saying. It can also look clumsy to fiddle with bits of paper over the OHP. If you do decide to use this approach it is better to place the masking sheet under the acetate, or to weight it down using a ruler or pen, as the OHP's glass top and internal fan frequently causes the masking sheet to slip out of position.

A technique, that has more or less been superseded by PowerPoint, is the use of overlays. Here several acetate sheets can be placed one on top of the other to build up the complexity of an image in a series of explained steps. Probably three or four overlays are the most that can be successfully managed. This process has transferred very effectively to PowerPoint presentations when the same slide can be shown several times in sequence with a little more information added each time. To the observer it looks as though things are appearing on the original image (see Figure 5.4).

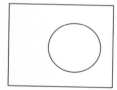

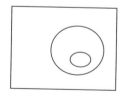

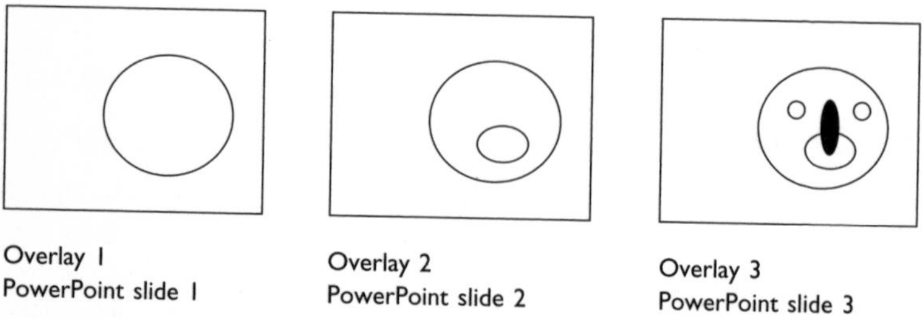

FIGURE 5.4 Using overhead transparency overlays

Designing overheads

The purpose of any visual aid is to help make a communication clearer and to help students understand and retain information and ideas, so keep the design simple, uncluttered and to the point.

Colours

Dark colours like black, blue and brown are easier to read on an acetate slide; use paler colours to underline or emphasize points. Some people prefer white text on a dark blue background and this has been a favoured colour combination for professionally produced projection slides. Remember, some students will be colour blind and they may confuse reds/greens and yellows/blues.

The three key points to consider with your colours are that they must blend well together, they must be readable on the screen and they must match the tone of your lecture's message and material. Clearly bright, lively colours may not be appropriate for a lecture on bereavement counselling and it is important to choose the colours that convey the appropriate message.

> Using red in a financial presentation to impress upon the audience your stability and prosperousness doesn't work. Red has the image of danger – being in the red.
>
> (Claudyne Wilder, founder of 'Wilder Presentations', Boston, USA, who trains professionals from the public and private sector on the design of spoken presentations)

Words

If in doubt make them bigger – nobody ever complains that it's too large to read. Use at least font size 24 and use a clear simple font without frills. Some believe sans serif fonts, such as Arial, are the easiest for students to read, particularly if they are partially sighted. Use a mix of upper and lower case when you write – again it is easier to read. Finally, always check your spelling.

Design

The most important aspect here is not to overpack your slides with too much information. The advice is no more than seven or eight lines of large clear text.

Using visuals

Use clipart, graphics, diagrams and other incorporated images to add interest. There are many advantages to using pictures/photos and graphics within a presentation:

- They can enhance understanding of a complicated idea or process.
- They can grab and keep attention.
- They aid memory – it is far easier for a student to remember a visual explanation than a series of words.
- They can be entertaining and help create a relaxed and positive atmosphere.

The importance of using graphics in visual aids to assist learning was investigated by Lee and Bowers (1997) – see Table 5.2.

TABLE 5.2 An investigation into the use of graphics in visual aids

Lee and Bowers studied a group of 112 university students to determine in which of the following conditions their students learnt best:

- reading printed text alone
- listening to spoken text alone
- looking at graphics alone
- listening to spoken text plus reading printed text
- listening to spoken text plus looking at graphics
- reading printed text plus looking at graphics
- listening to spoken text, reading printed text and looking at graphics.

The students sat a pre-test, then learnt the material, and then sat a post-test. Their post-test results were compared with those of a control group that took the same pre- and post-tests, but studied a different topic in between.

When compared with the control group, the performance of the people in the test groups was always better. The percentage increase for each learning condition is shown below.

Learning condition	% increase in results
Hearing spoken text and looking at graphics	91
Looking at graphics alone	63
Reading printed text plus looking at graphics	56
Listening to spoken text, reading text, and looking at graphics	46
Hearing spoken text plus reading printed text	32
Reading printed text alone	12
Hearing printed text alone	7

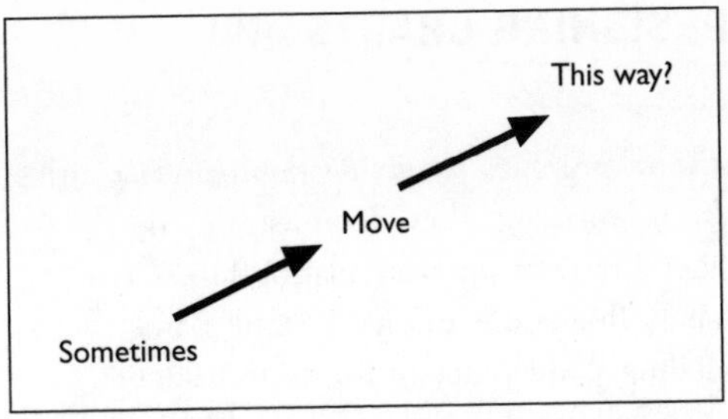

FIGURE 5.5 Diagram showing an example of a different viewing pathway of material/information presented on a slide

The results from this study suggest that the incorporation of graphics in visual aids will greatly assist learning.

If you have a choice don't always use the same slide templates for every lecture as this does tend to make one slide look very much like another and blur one into the next. Some universities and colleges do, however, recommend the use of a 'corporate design template'. A 'template' is the term used in PowerPoint presentation software to describe the different background designs for every slide including such things as; the colour scheme, the style of headings and borders etc. However, to give a professional impression, many lecturers try to keep the template consistent within any one lecture. You may also want to keep the format of any animation the same too, for example the way one slide is replaced by the next when you press 'next slide' in PowerPoint. If that is the case it is important to set a 'slide master'. Information that you wish to be present on every slide you present should also be set on the master, e.g. your name, logo, copyright details etc. (For more on the use of PowerPoint see below.)

Some presenters talk about planning a journey for the eye, and then try to design their visual aids with this in mind. Because of western writing convention the expected visual route over a slide is from the top left-hand corner through to the bottom right. Occasionally changing that 'journey' will have impact (see Figure 5.5).

Using bullet points can be an effective strategy for summarizing important information and can provide a helpful prompt to the lecturer who can use the listed points as triggers and expand upon them. However, turning all visual aids into bulleted lists is a mistake and if you spend a whole day watching PowerPoint conference presentations it will strongly reaffirm the need to avoid 'death by bullet point'.

QUICK ADVICE ON DESIGNING CHARTS AND GRAPHS

- Highlight the purpose of graphics by giving them precise titles that explain both the relationship they demonstrate and the conclusion the speaker draws from that relationship. Give titles to axes and label all sections of charts, tables and diagrams, thus modelling good practice for your students.
- Consider what kind of relationship you wish to demonstrate when choosing how to represent it. (Line graphs represent changes of a dependent variable as a function of changes in an independent variable, bar graphs represent relative quantities, pie charts show relative proportions of a whole etc.).
- It is difficult to get information out of a table quickly. Highlight significant numbers, convert data into graphic form or present minimal data to ease the audience's interpretation of a table.
- Minimize the amount of visual information the audience must process so that they can focus on the most important material.
- Make all print large enough for audience members to read comfortably – even if they are sitting in the back row with less than 20/20 vision.

DESIGNING A POWERPOINT PRESENTATION FOR USE WITH A DATA PROJECTOR

I wonder how you get that effect?

All of the above points of guidance apply – but some points should be applied with even greater stringency when using PowerPoint with a data projector. For example, eight lines of text on a projected PowerPoint slide are too many and five lines of text is a better maximum.

PowerPoint software offers a range of facilities for fading or emerging text, moving it in from the left or right, spiralling it up or dropping it down. Frequently these presentation effects can actually detract from the main message being communicated and they should be used with care and in moderation.

Where PowerPoint comes into its own as a presentation medium is when it is used to display things that would be very difficult or impossible to show using overhead projectors and other more traditional means. Being able to show, for example, an animation depicting how a turbine works, or how a virus enters a cell or how a pyramid may have been constructed, can save the lecturer many words and a lot of time. It is likely to be better understood, too. The incorporation of moving images, video clips and movie footage has brought to life and illustrated learning points in lectures in subjects as diverse as medicine, business studies and geography as well as in the more expected film study course.

The technology offers many possibilities. Teachers can plot graphs of data collected in class, and manipulate images in front of the students. Lecturers can link to information sites on the Internet to display materials, or link to 'online' discussions, or consult virtually and at a distance, with experts working in other universities. More on this later (see Chapter 8).

When not to use PowerPoint

Behind the suggestion given above for the use of PowerPoint lies an implicit 'don't'. Don't use PowerPoint simply to reproduce your OHP slides just because the equipment is there. You are not gaining anything for greater risk. It is more likely to go wrong technically; you might have to dim the lights to show the slides clearly, which is soporific and it is more difficult to be flexible and responsive to audience questions and interaction.

For example,

> Can I just ask you about the graph you showed five minutes ago and ask how it relates to the table you are now showing?

Such a question might cause difficulty for a PowerPoint user, but the OHP presenter can shuffle slides and respond much more easily.

SUMMARY

The availability of a wide range of visual aids to support the spoken delivery of a lecture is now commonplace. Selecting the most appropriate resource is important and new teachers should take the opportunity to explore and practise the use of different modes of delivery to expand their skills and gain confidence in the use of the equipment and technology. However, this exploration should be fundamentally driven by the learning goals and learning outcomes of a lecture and not trends and fashions.

EXAMPLES FROM DIFFERENT DISCIPLINES

There is considerable diversity in 'cultural norms' when it comes to selecting the most appropriate visual aids in a lecture. These are reflected in the following comments:

Engineering

> It wouldn't cross my mind not to use PowerPoint in my lectures. It looks professional, the students expect it and it is quick and easy for me to update.
>
> (Senior lecturer In the engineering department)

American and Canadian studies

> We just about have overhead projectors in the teaching rooms, I have no idea when we might see projection equipment.
>
> (Part-time tutor in American and Canadian studies)

Art history

> I still use my slides and the slide projector. I have tried putting them into a PowerPoint presentation but the clarity of the images isn't good enough.
>
> (Lecturer in art history)

Accountancy and finance

> Board work is central to how we teach in my department and I think it works well. I liked to see worked solutions when I was a student. There is something about seeing it done in front of you which is much more effective than just having the solution presented to you.
>
> (Postgraduate tutor in accountancy and finance)

FURTHER READING

Baume, D. and Baume, C. (1998) 'Learning to teach: making presentations', in Oxford Centre for Staff Development, *Training Materials for Research Students*. Oxford: OCSD.

Chin, P. (2004) *Using C&IT to Support Teaching*. London: RoutledgeFalmer.

Reece, I. and Walker, S. (1995) *A Practical Guide to the Overhead Projector and Other Visual Aids*. Sunderland: Business Education Publishers.

Woolsey, J. D. (1989) 'Combating poster fatigue: how to use visual grammar and analysis to effect better visual communications', *Trends in Neurosciences*, 12: 325–32.

USEFUL WEB SITES

http://www.aare.edu.au/01pap/ho01072.htm Ho, B. (2001) 'From using transparencies to using PowerPoint slides in the classroom', Australian Association for Research in Education (AARE) Conference proceedings.

http://www.presentersuniversity.com/courses/show_vadesigning.cfm?RecordID=88 For a range of interesting articles on the design and use of PowerPoint presentations see the audio-visual aids section of the Presenter's University website.

http://www.sas.upenn.edu/cwic/resources.html Communication Within the Curriculum (CwiC) is a University of Pennsylvania program that supports student speaking as a means of both communicating and learning. The CwiC website provides a wide range of resources to support oral communication.

Chapter 6

Active learning in interactive lectures

INTRODUCTION

In this chapter the authors wish to encourage lecturers to use a variety of mechanisms to enrich the learning experience of their students in the lecture theatre. Sitting, listening and taking notes for hour after hour is very difficult to do (remember how it feels at the end of a full day of lectures when you attend a conference?). We are not suggesting that a lecture should be scripted like a James Bond film but it should contain different movements, it should include different presentation modalities and it should appeal to the senses in as many ways as possible. There are a number of simple ways that the stimulus can be varied from the presentation point of view. Simply splitting a lecture into context, content and closure as described in Chapter 4 is already one way of modulating the overall experience. In order to increase attention span, engage the students and encourage them to think, it is also recommended that the lecturer considers breaking the lecture into short sub-sections of 'lecturer input' and interspersing this with student activities that provide opportunities for active learning and interaction.

Why use interactive lectures?
http://www.swap.ac.uk/learning/Interactive

They enable the lecturer to:

- find out students' starting point
- challenge students
- check assumptions
- link sessions throughout a unit/module.

Interactive lectures may help student learning as they can:

- keep students awake and warmed up!
- open students' receptivity
- accustom students to having a voice
- help students absorb information
- help students with a variety of learning styles
- aid retention of learning through articulation of views.

Students can also view the introduction of active learning approaches in lectures positively. Studies in the early 1990s reported that the students consulted found a traditional, didactic lecture to be their least favourite form of teaching (Butler 1992). Williams (1992) also reports that her students were willing and enthusiastic about taking a more active role in the lecture.

Many students say that they enjoy interactive lectures more than a traditional didactic lecture. Some also report that they feel that they learn more:

It forces me to think during the lecture.

Yes, it's a good idea. I do learn more than in a normal lecture.

I think that feedback and interaction is always beneficial because more ideas and perspectives are brought out and argued. The interaction forces you to apply the theory and more fully understand the material or clarify what you don't understand.

Yes, I do learn more, in terms of expanding my thinking on concepts by hearing points of view that I wouldn't have thought of. Also, speaking with the lecturer removes the 'power' dynamic of authoritative teacher and a powerless, voiceless student.

Interaction provides communication between students and enables them/us to be informed in topics we're too shy to ask about.

(Views of sociology students attending interactive lectures reported in Crowe and Pemberton 2002)

DOES INTERACTIVE LECTURING AID LEARNING?

Does it work better? Do students understand material more deeply and remember it for longer? Do they do better in their exams? Many teachers have explored the use of interactive lecturing and come to their own decisions. The literature is littered with examples of teachers and course designers evaluating their own provision and trying to assess the effectiveness of this way of teaching.

Many teachers report a positive response to the introduction of active learning approaches in their lectures.

> We are venturing to say that coming to grips with the material in the classroom, where the student is committed via small group exercises, and other active strategies, to 'owning' the material, turns the student into an active, more effective learner, who is more likely to achieve the learning outcomes of the lecture. If that is so, however, we would expect that not only would students prefer to answer exam questions based on material they felt more comfortable with, they actually would perform better – i.e. achieve higher grades – on those questions.
>
> This is precisely what we found. Although it is 'early days' yet to argue in any other than a tentative way, the results of the use of the interactive lecture format are encouraging.
>
> (Crowe and Pemberton 2000)

However, proving that changing one aspect of teaching in a large and complex curriculum is beneficial for all the students in a diverse class is clearly very difficult to do. There are so many variables and potential points of bias. Some students enjoy a more participatory way of learning and therefore engage more fully with the ideas and material of the course, while others would much prefer just to be told what to write down in their notes to pass the examination. So how do we try to measure the success of a teaching strategy? We could interview students to find out how much they rate the effectiveness, or look at rates of attendance at classes, compare performance in examinations, record students' future course choices and expressions of interest in the subject in the future? There are many valid questions that we can use to build up a picture of teaching effectiveness for our own courses.

We also cannot avoid thinking about the different learning styles and expectations of our students. The charisma and skills of the lecturer will also have a significant part to play and impact on the students' experiences and preferences. In short, absolute proof of impact is difficult to obtain, cause and effect being notoriously difficult to pin down in a multi-variable experimental condition. However, the number of articles supporting the introduction of active learning methods in lectures and reporting the positive experiences on individual courses by individual lecturers are collectively building a very persuasive argument in favour of this way of lecturing.

Personal choices

Clearly the number of students in the lecture, the venue, the topic and the teaching style and preferences of the lecturer will determine the frequency and appropriateness of the learning activities incorporated. Teachers new to lecturing may well wish to 'build up' their confidence and teaching skills and begin their exploration of active learning in lectures modestly by using some of the techniques described in this chapter, if possible, beginning with smaller scale activities, with smaller classes, in favourable environments. However, the ideal is not always possible and the luxury of the 'developmental and incremental approach' may be denied some new teachers because they have relatively few opportunities to lecture (particularly new part-time teachers).

Why not?

Bonwell and Eison (1991) have identified a number of barriers to incorporating active learning into a lecture. These include the impact of educational tradition and breaking with the norm that may lead to a lack of support from colleagues and departments. We have already mentioned the reaction from some students who would apparently prefer a more didactic and passive lecture. Perhaps the most significant barrier is that of personal risk which can take many forms. Will I lose control of the class? Will I fail? Will the students give me bad student reports if I try asking them questions in the lecture? Will my colleagues think that I am not teaching properly and reneging on my responsibilities? Table 6.1 presents responses to many of the common criticisms and difficulties raised when considering introducing active learning in lectures.

There is no doubt that lecturing in this way does require particular skills from the lecturer and changes the role of the teacher. As with

TABLE 6.1 Introducing 'active learning' in lectures: common challenges and possible ways forward

Challenge	Response?
'Interaction reduces the time for content delivery'	Most lectures are overloaded and reducing input may be helpful and actually increase learning
'Students just want a good set of lecture notes to learn later'	Interactivity does not preclude this and the lecturer can still provide clear and structured lecture notes
'The lecture is where we tell the students things'	Using interaction will let you know that the students have heard and understood what you have told them
'The students will hate it and won't take part'	The teaching approach may need to be explained and the activities justified in terms of the intended learning goals
'The students don't know enough to be able to talk about it yet'	The choice of learning task is crucial – talking about it may not be appropriate, but applying a new concept might
'What if they ask me things that I can't answer?'	Good – it shows they are thinking, and this is not a personal challenge; students can be referred to other sources and topics can be revisited in later sessions or via course VLEs
'They might just be discussing last night's football'	Give a clear focus, timescale and endpoint to the task and move around the classroom to monitor activities and very few students will wander off course
'Won't the lecture just lose clarity?'	As with the didactic lecture a clear structure is needed, the map should be shared with the students at the outset and a balance should be maintained between input and interaction

small group teaching (see Exley and Dennick 2004) the lecturer is now faced with the responsibility of constructing appropriate interactions and responding to students' comments and feedback. Just as the skills of presenting are developed through practice and reviewing successes and weaknesses, so are the skills of coordinating interactions in the lecture. New teachers can learn from others and gain ideas from this chapter but should be prepared to learn as they go, building confidence and a personal belief in this approach.

What can I do?

If persuaded to give active learning in lectures a try there are fundamentally three ways in which the lecturer can vary what the students do in a lecture:

- what the students hear
- what the students see
- what the students do (on their own and in groups).

This chapter is constructed around these three dimensions and focuses on the student experience in the class.

VARYING WHAT THE STUDENTS CAN HEAR IN A LECTURE

The lecturer's voice is clearly the most important thing that students will hear. As a common complaint from students is a monotone projection it is crucial for lecturers to modulate their voice by varying pitch and intensity to stress and highlight points, to pause for emphasis and take natural breaks in speech to help the students listen effectively and keep their attention. (See Chapter 5 for a fuller discussion of the use and care of the voice.)

Audio recordings

In a number of disciplines it may be very useful for the students to hear examples of soundbites and audiotaped recordings to illustrate the points being presented, for example sounds made by different bird species in ecology/biology, heart murmurs in medicine, or instrument signals in astronomy. In other subjects it may be very informative and stimulating for the students to hear radio samples, for example an interview with a politician, an orchestral conductor or a business woman.

Teachers may make their own recordings to demonstrate particular learning points. These may be 'real' or 'simulated', for example a conversation between a dentist and patient or a marketing director and client. The power of the isolated spoken word, undiluted by visual images, can be a very powerful trigger for thinking. It may give more space for individual interpretation and creativity and be more easily anonymized, if it is important to protect an individual's confidentiality.

Occasionally lecturers may play music in a lecture. This may be the topic of the lecture or to reinforce a point being made. Alternatively it may be used to give the students a break and a rest from concentrating and note taking. This is more likely during longer, two- or three-hour lecture slots or during evening teaching sessions when part-time students are studying after work.

VARYING WHAT THE STUDENTS CAN SEE IN A LECTURE

The students will see the lecturer first and it may be possible to vary this through team teaching and through the use of 'lecture duets' (Somers and Campbell, 1996). Hearing two different perspectives on a topic or staging a semi-structured debate can really bring a subject to life and help convey the complexity and diversity of the topic.

Guest lecturers

Several teaching courses make extensive use of 'guest lecturers'. These may be specialists, professionals, industrialists, etc. who are asked to contribute their particular knowledge or experience in the field to broaden a fundamentally academic position. However, the course leader should take great care to brief their guests properly and clearly explain what is expected of them – preferably in writing. Details such as the timings of the lecture, the focus and learning outcomes, the range and scope wanted should be specified. The students' academic background and information about their prior experience, level of understanding and context of learning should also be explained to the speaker. In order for the lecture course to remain coherent and retain some consistency, the course leader could also helpfully discuss issues of teaching style and expected norms in the lecture. These courses can often be experienced by the students as a series of unlinked talking heads and leave them feeling insecure about their future assessments. The coordinating role is therefore crucial.

Using visual aids

Many lecturers use a variety of visual aids and presentation tools to get their message across. The use of overhead projectors, visualizers, slide projectors, flipcharts, white/blackboards, interactive whiteboards and smartboards and PowerPoint were discussed in detail in Chapter 5. One comment here is the reminder that the use of different visual aids will bring very different classroom dynamics and student expectations. For example, the use of PowerPoint echoes the style of a professional presentation and students report finding such a lecture virtually impossible to interrupt with questions. It feels more formal.

Body language

> Whether we choose to ignore the body or to highlight it, the fact of the matter is that it is important to know that we speak volumes about ourselves through it, whether we know it or not. Erving Goffman would comment that, while an individual can stop speaking, he or she cannot stop communicating, through body idiom. You can say the right thing or the wrong thing with the body, but you cannot say nothing.
>
> (MacNevin 2000)

There are several (non-evidenced) estimates that suggest as much as 70 per cent of communication is non-verbal and in one-to-one communication a more detailed breakdown of percentages gives 7 per cent in words, 23 per cent in the tone of voice, 35 per cent in facial expression and 35 per cent in body language. Even if these figures are generally assertions in the literature the message is clear. The lecturer's thoughts will definitely affect his or her tone of voice, facial expression and body language. Feelings of boredom or frustration will show through the lecturer, be implicitly interpreted by the students and impact strongly on their experience of the lecture.

Body language and its interpretation also differ between countries and cultures. In the world of business a great deal of effort has been spent in trying to improve understanding of the ways in which cultural body language differs. In teaching too, lecturers will wish to avoid unnecessarily offending their students and may find it difficult to interpret correctly the non-verbal feedback they receive from some international students during the lecture.

TABLE 6.2 Using demonstrations in lectures

Demonstration type	Examples of practice
Model a skill or a procedure	Show how to take a blood pressure measurement; show how to play a chord on a guitar
Display a sample or example	Pass round the class a piece of sandstone to compare it with a piece of marble. Bring into class original manuscripts
Use a model to explain an abstract or complex idea	Bend a piece of wired string to show how DNA is packaged in the nucleus; ask the class to do a Mexican wave to illustrate nerve synapses
Ask students to demonstrate to themselves through personal experience	To experience skeletal muscle fatigue while repeatedly clenching and unclenching a fist; to view images that can be interpreted in a variety of ways
Present an actual or simulated situation or case study	Show the company mission statements and policy documents; use the real brief given to the contracting architects; ask a nurse to take a patient's history

Demonstrations

A demonstration basically involves showing the students something. You can choose to show a range of things in a lecture for a variety of educational purposes. Some examples are given in Table 6.2.

Using video clips

As with audiotaped recordings, video clips can provide a different and stimulating way of bringing material into the lecture for discussion. Videos may be professionally produced teaching or training videos that are bought to be presented in class. It is also reasonably common practice to use homemade video clips or recordings for teaching sessions. However, there are complex issues of copyright that need to be considered.

Copyright is the exclusive right that protects an author, composer, producer or programmer from having work reproduced or exhibited publicly without expressed permission. Many universities have entered into licence agreements that enable teachers to make use of TV and radio programmes for the purposes of education and assessment. The purpose must be for educational, not promotional or recreational use, and the (non-paying) audience must be registered students and staff.

Several universities will hold the ERA (Educational Recording Agency) Licence that is a blanket licence that allows reasonably free use of TV material for teaching. You can record feature films, advertisements, documentaries, dramas, etc. You can also record cable and satellite programmes as there isn't, as yet, a licensing scheme in place to cover their use.

Please note that programmes and resources produced by the Open University are not included under the ERA Licence but are covered by a separate licence agreement. Again, many universities do hold this licence.

It is very important that new teachers consult with experts on copyright law and the licence agreements held by their own institution before copying and showing clips.

VARYING WHAT THE STUDENTS CAN DO INDIVIDUALLY IN A LECTURE

With very large classes in unsympathetic environments the best way of encouraging students to interact with the ideas and material of the lecture may be to set them individual tasks to carry out during the class.

The most commonly used approach is simply to ask the students a question and ask them to think about it for a few moments and try to respond. Here lies the first big decision for the lecturer.

Do you want to know the answers that the students have come up with? It may be important for you to hear their responses and feedback for several reasons:

- to encourage more students to participate in the activity in the first place
- to demonstrate that the answers they generate are useful and important

- to check that the students are understanding the lecture so far
- to identify and be able to correct misunderstandings
- to help you shape what you say next.

On the other hand it may not be important to get feedback during the class. The purpose of the task may be that the students can check their own understanding, or to prompt thinking and deeper learning, and in this circumstance feedback is not essential. Or, the task may be included in the lecture simply to add variety in the learning process and to give the students a break from listening and note taking and so help them maintain their concentration when the lecturer later resumes his or her presentation.

Whether or not the lecturer feels it is important to hear back from the students after they have completed a task will depend utterly on the intended purpose of the activity.

Central to a lecturer's decision is the notion that any time that students spend on individual or group activities in the lecture is effectively 'bought' with time the lecturer could be spending in traditional didactic delivery. So, the purpose of the activity should be clear to the lecturer. In some 'content-heavy' disciplines shifting the 'input/activity' balance may seem more difficult to justify as it may not represent the norm.

(Please see the section 'Hearing back from the students' (page 96) for further ideas about how to manage class feedback.)

Tasks for individual students

Asking questions

Many lecturers ask their students questions in their lectures but frequently comment that they find it very difficult to get their students to answer. When asking questions give the students thinking time, ask them to write down their answers and if possible set a target that will stretch your students. For example:

> Please write down at least five good reasons why we use lectures in higher education? Be prepared to justify your answer.
>
> Make a quick note of as many meanings for the word set as you can. You should be able to come up with at least four.

TABLE 6.3 Tasks which students can undertake in a lecture

Students can be asked to:

- search for, select and organize information supplied
- abbreviate, or summarize information supplied
- solve problems and answer questions
- set problems and ask questions
- make a judgement on a case or a situation
- predict the outcome of an experiment or an intervention
- estimate the cost of a design choice or a business decision
- make a diagnosis
- list and prioritize.

What else can we ask students to do in a lecture? Table 6.3 provides a summary of ideas for activities.

Timing

The positioning of student learning activities in the sequence of the lecture is also worth considering here. Let us take the example of a 'quiz'.

The use of quizzes in a lecture can serve several different roles for the lecturer (and students). At the very beginning of the class a quiz on the content of the previous week's lecture can help the students remember what was being discussed in the last class and help to link the content to this week's lecture. It can help the class quickly settle to the work of this week's lecture and may be used to highlight areas of weakness or help the lecturer emphasize that there is still much to learn about the topic, if the students already feel that they know all there is to learn on the matter!

Using a quiz, twenty minutes in, can provide the change of pace and the different learning activity that can help the students to concentrate and focus on the topic. The quiz questions can be used to check understanding and to see if the students can indeed apply what they have just heard about, whether that be ideas, theories or principles.

At the very end of the lecture a quiz can act as a 'live summary' of the key points that the lecturer wishes to emphasize. It may act as a checking mechanism to focus the students and force their detailed attention. It may also serve as a vehicle for linking today's lecture with next week's – and highlight the 'questions' that the next class will address.

FIGURE 6.1 'Hello back there'

Hearing back from the students

If it is important to gather the ideas and views from students in the lecture there are a number of ways that the lecturer may tackle this. Voting is probably the simplest method: 'Who thinks left . . . who thinks right . . . who isn't sure?' There is a natural resistance to voting; students may be inhibited from expressing their views in public and exposing their ignorance, or they may simply feel silly sticking their hand in the air. Teachers may use voting repeatedly in a lecture and so erode some of this resistance and encourage more students to take an active role. The show of hands can be replaced by other forms of voting, for example students could be asked to stand up before the question is asked and then either sit down (to indicate a 'Yes' vote) or remain standing (for a 'No' vote) to express their views. To energize a tired class this physical movement is a good thing.

Providing handouts with different, contrasting, coloured front and back sheets allows the students to vote by showing the different colour – this 'all at once' system of voting has advantages because it is obvious who is abstaining and the lecturer can focus his or her attention on encouraging the non-participants.

To obtain fuller responses from the students it is helpful to provide very clear instructions to the class about what you are wanting from them, for example: 'In two minutes I will be asking you to give me at least five reasons why we assess undergraduates.' Then student views can be sampled. Suggestions can be requested from students sitting in different parts of the lecture theatre: 'Can I have one reason from your list? Let's take one from over here' (indicating with your hands and eye contact). The students sitting in this section of the room will feel more obliged to respond to you but you are avoiding putting any one individual on the spot.

A concern

Picking on individual students to answer a question is a high-risk strategy that will increase the tension in the classroom. If the chosen student doesn't know the answer, or answers incorrectly, the lecturer has the difficulty of rescuing the situation. He or she must try not to embarrass the student further while providing the rest of the class with the correct answer clearly. The student selected may be painfully shy or have a disability that affects his or her ability to communicate when under pressure. The authors suggest that this method only be used when the lecturer knows the class well and has developed a certain rapport with the students which enables him/her to respond with appropriate tact and sensitivity to the class atmosphere.

It may be appropriate to ask students for written responses or feedback. The lecturer can pass post-it notes around the class and ask them to write their feedback and comments on them (individually or in small groups). This approach is more commonly used in small group teaching but in smaller sized lectures it may be a useful method to collect views on the topic, on the teacher, on the course, etc. Race (1999) suggests that the use of post-its can encourage participation from students who are less confident and forthcoming in oral feedback sessions.

Some lecturers cut up overhead projector acetates into quarters, and pass the quarters and pens around the lecture theatre, asking the students to make their contributions if they wish. Not all students can make their comments known in this way but it does provide some sampling of views and ideas to be included in the class. Advantages of this report-back method are that lecturers can preview and think about, the contributions before showing them to the class. They can show up to four comments at once which will allow them to draw comparisons, indicate differences of opinion, relate ideas to each other, etc. The comments are effectively anonymous in a lecture of any size and, therefore, lecturers may also feel freer to critique the contributions without directly criticizing the contributor.

The use of interactive handsets in lectures is currently being explored and tested in several universities (Draper 2003). Using the same technology as TV remote control buttons, these handsets provide a means of gaining feedback from every student. Students use their own keypad (hand held or inset into the chairs or desks) to respond to the lecturer's questions, vote or express opinions. The class responses are fed into a computer and the group response calculated before the information is projected onto the screen in the lecture theatre. For further discussion of the use of this technology see Chapter 8.

Using incomplete handouts

For large lectures the incomplete handout provides the opportunity to give written instructions about learning tasks, very clearly, to a large number of students. Instructions are more likely to be misheard or misinterpreted when just given orally to large groups.

The structure of the task can be set out clearly with appropriate gaps and spaces in which the students can make notes and give their answers. When taking lecture notes it is very likely that students will not record the learning that takes place during discussion activities or learning tasks so this work is frequently lost from the written record of the lecture i.e. the students' lecture notes. Failure to make notes supports the notion that the learning that takes place through the interactive parts of the lecture is less important and less valid that that gained through the lecturer's direct input. By designing lecture handouts that incorporate student learning activities in the form of 'worksheets' it is more likely that students will leave the lecture with a fuller and more complete record of their learning experience.

TABLE 6.4 Suggested learning activities for students using interactive handouts in lectures

Students working with interactive handouts can be asked to:

- complete a picture
- complete passages of text
- complete definitions, formulae, etc.
- draw up lists
- draw a graph
- label a graph
- fill in values in a table
- correct the errors in a calculation, a translation, a music score, etc.
- interpret the experimental results provided
- annotate or label a diagram
- put arrows on a flow chart
- plot positions on a map
- represent information as a pie chart, bar chart, etc.

The tasks that can be incorporated into interactive handouts may include those presented in Table 6.4 (the tasks suggested for individual students in Table 6.3 could also be very readily incorporated into a handout).

Some teachers have found that an interactive handout can become the structuring focus for an entire lecture. (See Chapter 7 for more detail about the use of handouts and examples of practice.)

VARYING WHAT THE STUDENTS CAN DO IN PAIRS AND SMALL GROUPS IN A LECTURE

Many of the individual activities described above can be extended to include an additional step in which the students are asked to discuss their views with a neighbour. Peer interaction leads to valuable learning outcomes (Biggs 1999a). Through discussion, students may clarify their thinking because they have to organize their thoughts to put them into words. They may have their views challenged or questioned and so be better prepared to defend and justify their positions. They practise giving their opinions out loud, finding the right words to express themselves clearly and gain experience in using the language of the discipline. All these factors mean that students are usually more willing to share their thoughts with a wider group, with the class as a whole, following a discussion in pairs. This may, therefore, be a prerequisite for the broader discussion or plenary session that follows a particular learning task.

It has been shown (Nicol and Boyle 2003) that asking students to think about a question individually before going into a discussion with colleagues nearby is very beneficial. It is more likely that all students will take an active part in the discussion and less likely that a few will dominate. This clearly has the potential to increase the quality of exchanges.

When asking students to discuss their views the lecturer can vary the directions given. For example, he or she may say:

- Compare your list with your neighbour.
- Interview your neighbour about his or her list.
- Look for interesting differences between you and your neighbour.
- Reach a consensus with your neighbour.
- Combine yours and your neighbour's lists and prioritize the top three.

How big can you go?

Pair work is the easiest to manage in very large lectures in fixed seating lecture theatres. However, if desirable, it is possible to ask one pair to turn around and talk to the pair behind them. Asking students to get out of their seats and perch on their desks may be a helpful thing to do if the students have been sitting for a long time. However, it is clearly disruptive and time-consuming to ask students to move around too much in such a room. At a stretch groups of up to six can be formed by asking three students in two adjacent rows to work together. In a room with a level floor and moveable furniture larger groups can work together, although the optimal group size for discussion is about six and discussion becomes more difficult above eight.

> If you have the potential to organize your lectures in a more flexible manner and can arrange for the students to be sitting and working in small groups during the class, you may find Chapter 9, on Workshops and Syndicate Groups, useful in the 'Small Group Teaching' volume of this series (Exley and Dennick 2004.)

Dealing with the consequences

If you encourage interaction and discussion in your class and, by design, try to make your students braver so that they can feed back and respond to your questions, there will be other consequences too. The traditional power balances shift; students may be more likely to interrupt you and ask questions and challenge your perspective. Some may enjoy being controversial (Stefani 2001) while others, few in number, may seek to be disruptive.

When using group working in the lecture there is also the problem of having to facilitate many small groups simultaneously and control the overall activity and noise level. These problems can be solved by judicious organization. It is usually not a problem for students to talk in twos and threes but students do need to be persuaded to get into these groups and there is always a tendency for them to try to stick to friendship groups.

The lecturer shouldn't be afraid to walk out into the lecture theatre and walk up and down the aisles making sure students have formed groups correctly and that they are on task. Clearly there will be a lot of noise but giving good, clear instructions, ensuring everyone knows what they are supposed to do and keeping strictly to time is the best way to manage these activities.

What can be achieved in such groupings? Essentially anything that might be achieved in a small group teaching situation. However, the groups might focus on a task requiring the use of an interactive handout. There might be some sort of output needed from each group: an answer to a problem, a list or a definition. Students might read them out or they might be collected on an overhead and displayed at the end. Not all groups need to do the same task and the room might be divided up into specific groups.

IN SUMMARY

By combining the active and interactive techniques described above a lecture can be turned into more than just the transmission of information. Not only will it be a much more stimulating and possibly memorable activity but it will also allow students genuinely to do things rather than merely follow the lecturer doing things. This will enable some of the higher level cognitive outcomes, such as applying knowledge and problem solving, to be achieved.

EXAMPLES FROM DIFFERENT DISCIPLINES

Mathematics

I sometimes give the students a handout which contains a worked example of the method that I have just explained to them in the first half of the lecture. I ask them to write a similar question (this usually involves the students in swapping numbers in my original). I give them a couple of minutes to do this then ask them to exchange questions with a person sitting near them in the lecture. They then try to solve their partner's question. They then pass it back to the question writer to be marked. This means that during the class they are asked to work through two examples (their own and their partner's) and the students are likely to do this as it involves showing their work to other people.

(Based on discussions with a lecturer in maths)

Geography

I am new to teaching and the only active learning approach I have tried so far is getting the students to vote whether they agree or disagree with points that I present or simple yes/no questions. The first few times I tried this many of the students abstained and didn't vote either way. I have found that the more you ask them to vote the more people will take part. I am tempted to try 'reverse voting', i.e. ask everybody to raise their hands in the first place and to show their voting preference by lowering their hands – I think there is something difficult about making that first move that stops some students from voting.

(Based on discussions with a new teacher in geography)

Health care

I usually use a buzz group in my lectures, just to break things up for the students. I ask quick questions that are intended to make my students link what I am talking about with their experiences on the ward or in practice. It is very important that the relevance of the theory is clear to my students; many are mature students who actually feel very under-confident in the classroom. I think the informality of a buzz group makes some of them feel more comfortable. If I have asked them to draw up a quick list of factors that can contribute to heart disease, I may simply ask for a few suggestions from the group and a few bolder students will shout things out. Another way I sometimes handle this is to put up a list of the contributing factors on PowerPoint and ask them to give themselves a mark for everyone they got – and then add the ones they missed to their notes. It depends how long I have got for class discussion.

(From a nurse practitioner in health care)

Electrical engineering

When I am explaining something complex and complicated, like the way current flows through a particular circuit, I use a diagram technique which seems to work quite well. First I explain the principles to the students and then I show them a diagram which needs to be completed and annotated by drawing arrows or '+' or '–' signs to show the direction of the current. I give the students a handout with two small copies of this incomplete diagram and I ask them to have a go at completing the top diagram (either on their own or with a friend). I give them a couple of minutes to do this before putting up a correct and annotated version of the diagram on a slide. They can then check their own work and if they have made a hash of it they can copy down the right answer so they have a neat version for their notes and later revision. It makes the students think about what they are doing rather than just copying everything off the slides.

(Post-doctoral researcher in electrical engineering)

Medical education

I have found that traditionally students are reluctant to individually respond to questions in a large lecture theatre. The act of 'cold' pointing or asking serial questions along a row is anxiety-provoking and can be humiliating for some students. Students are often uncertain how to respond and fear a sarcastic remark from the lecturer or sniggers from their peers if wrong. The process actually inhibits any further interactivity.

However, if I prime the students and warm them up in some way then they can be more responsive. A friendly introduction, an acknowledgement of questioning anxiety and a promise that there are 'no stupid answers' can break the ice and encourage responses to questions addressed generally. Asking a question, allowing students to think about it for a minute and then discuss their answer with their neighbour will also have an 'ice-breaking' effect and will elicit better responses.

If students are reluctant to respond to questions individually I don't find that to be the case *en masse*. Students in general don't mind putting their hands up although they sometimes need a little bit of cajoling to make sure everyone is responding. Putting up one's hand can be used with conventional dichotomous (yes/no, true/false) questions or the multiple-choice variety. The lecturer should display the question on the screen, with the alternative responses, and then give the students a few moments to think and write down their choice. If this is then followed by: 'How many people think the answer is Yes, hands up', or 'How many people think the answer is 1, hands up', 'How many think it's 2', etc., a good response should be obtained.

(A lecturer in medical education)

FURTHER READING

Andreson, L. (1994) *Lecturing to Large Groups*, Staff and Educational Development Association Paper 81. Birmingham: Staff and Educational Development Association.

Biggs, J. (1999a) 'Enriching large-class teaching', in *Teaching for Quality Learning at University*. Buckingham: Society for Research into Higher Education and Open University Press.

Collett, Peter (2003) *The Book of Tells*. London: Bantam. (An up-to-date book on body language.)

Cown, J. (1998) 'How should I get started', in *On Becoming an Innovative University Teacher*. Buckingham: Society for Research into Higher Education and Open University Press.

Davies, P. (2003) *Practical Ideas for Enhancing Lectures*, Staff and Educational Development Association Special 13. Birmingham: Staff and Educational Development Association.

USEFUL WEB SITES

http://www.swap.ac.uk/learning/interactive1.asp The Social Policy and Social Work LTSN – SWAP website offers advice and suggestions on using interactive lecturing.

Interactive lectures

http://www.id.ucsb.edu/IC/Resources/Teaching/interactlecture.html Office of Instructional Consultation, University of California, Santa Barbara.

http://instruct1.cit.cornell.edu/courses/taresources/large.html *Add Active Learning to Large Classes, Resources for Scientists Teaching Science* website.

The Active Learning Site

http://www.active-learning-site.com/index.html The site provides an up-to-date bibliography of research articles on active learning and large class teaching.

Chapter 7

Handouts

INTRODUCTION

Handouts are paper-based resources given out before, during or after a lecture. In this chapter we wish to examine why handouts are used, to explore further uses for handouts and to look at what makes a good quality handout.

Handouts are used for essentially two reasons in lectures:

- to provide information
- to provide an opportunity for activity.

Using handouts as sources of information is their traditional function, whereas using handouts as vehicles for student activity is a relatively recent development, building on the concepts of active learning (see series website guide, Brown 2004). The different ways in which information handouts can be used are described and discussed below.

HANDOUTS AS INFORMATION

Full lecture notes

Handouts can be used to provide a printed version of a lecture, either as a summary or as copies of overheads produced by, for example, PowerPoint. They can also be used to provide extra information not given in the lecture.

Handouts that give a summary of key points, learning outcomes or an outline of the lecture

A handout might contain a condensed summary of the key ideas and concepts presented in a lecture. It might list the learning outcomes, an outline of the lecture's main headings and the conclusions reached. However, handouts can easily contain copies of all the overheads used, providing students with almost a complete record of the lecture.

Handouts like this are essentially just a printed version of the lecture without any additional information or added value and careful thought should be given to their potential effects on learning. An advantage of such handouts is that all students have access to the main concepts of the lecture, regardless of their note-taking ability or their language proficiency; the lecturer can be certain that the lecture has been 'covered'. This can be useful if students have missed lectures through illness or who have a disability affecting their ability to take notes. However, this approach can generate a 'spoon-feeding' attitude to teaching. Students will soon realize that everything they need to know is in the handout and that attending the lecture is not essential as long as they can get hold of a copy of the handout; lecture attendance might start to decline. This situation can be exacerbated if handouts are made available electronically via a Virtual Learning Environment where students can have access to lecture notes and presentation material prior to the lecture.

A 'spoon-feeding' attitude can be prevented if the availability of handouts means that students do not have to take extensive lecture notes and can concentrate on listening and thinking about the content and arguments in the lecture. The delivery of the lecture may even be altered by this approach, as the lecturer is now no longer concerned that students have to copy everything down. The lecturer should discuss the use of the handout with students and make it clear that, although the handout provides a record of the content of the lecture, attendance and listening to explanations is still important in comprehensive learning. Nevertheless, handouts can still be seen by students as just more 'other people's writing' to process and can be ignored.

Partial lecture notes

Handouts providing additional material

A modification of the previous approach is the provision of handouts that only contain certain essential elements of the lecture, which would take students too long to copy down, such as important diagrams, figures or tables.

Handouts providing more information than could be presented in the lecture

We have already discussed the problem of information overload in lectures and suggested that lectures with too much information become ineffective. Students can become overwhelmed with detail and time management can become a problem. A solution to this problem is to provide additional material in handouts to be read and processed after the lecture. Additional detail, problems and case studies can all be provided in this way. The lecturer can then concentrate on explaining key information during the lecture but know that the students all have copies of additional important and relevant material to take away. A common type of further information to provide is a list of further reading and references.

From a curriculum perspective it is important to recognize that the lecture and its associated handouts form the overall content for that session. Clearly this information should fit into the overall curriculum design of a course or module in a balanced way. Handouts should not become yet another way to overburden the student with too much material.

HANDOUTS FOR ACTIVITY

Although the use of handouts as a source of information can help learning if sensitively integrated into a lecture, by far the best use of handouts is as a tool for active learning. Information can still be provided but the handout should also contain spaces for a variety of activities involving the individual or group processing of information, application and problem solving. If the overall handout also ends up being a record of the key points of the lecture then so much the better. The use of interactive handouts also gives students a sense of ownership of the lecture as they insert definitions, label diagrams or insert their answers to questions.

The variety of activities that can be facilitated by using 'interactive handouts' is as wide as the imagination of the lecturer but some of the more common techniques are listed and described below. How these activities can be integrated into an 'active lecture' will also be described.

A case study using a two-page interactive handout in a lecture is described at the end of the chapter.

Gapped handouts

This is one of the simplest ways of encouraging interaction. The handout contains a piece of text with some key words left blank. The students have to fill it in, working out the correct words from their background knowledge and the context. It may seem a trivial task but do not overestimate the ability of students to deal with new words and terminology. The task can be made more interactive by asking students to vote by putting up their hand on the correct word from a list presented on an overhead.

Spaces for definitions, formulae, etc.

In the overall design of the interactive handout spaces can be left to insert important definitions, names, dates, formulae, etc. Students can be given a brief opportunity to fill them in or the lecturer can give them directly, depending on the situation.

Incomplete definitions, formulae, etc.

A variation on the previous method is to provide incomplete definitions or formulae that have to be completed by students.

Spaces for lists with headings

Some activities involve students thinking up lists, inserting words or completing chronologies. Partially drawn tables with subheadings or timelines can be provided to facilitate this process.

Spaces for graphs, diagrams, maps, flow charts, etc.

In some cases it is useful to leave a section of space for students to draw a diagram or a graph. Alternatively an unlabelled diagram can be provided that is labelled during the lecture or the axes of a graph can be provided ready for a graph to be inserted. This idea can be extended to maps, flow charts, concept trees or any other appropriate diagram.

Incomplete or unlabelled processes or sequences

In the scientific and technological disciplines there are many processes that can be described diagrammatically. These can be provided in outline form with spaces left for students to insert arrows or connectors between the elements. Alternatively the arrows can be provided and students have to fit in the components.

Problems with space for answers

Encouraging students to apply their knowledge can be facilitated by providing questions, problems, scenarios or 'case vignettes' that are worked on during the session, leaving spaces for students to insert their answers. Questions can be inserted testing previous knowledge and understanding during the lecture and providing a brief test at the end.

Interactive handouts

Some or all of the above methods can be incorporated into an interactive handout, and examples are shown in Figures 7.1 and 7.2. However, the structure and sequencing of sections in the handout needs to be carefully integrated with the overall structure of the lecture. If students are to take away an overview of the lecture then the completed handout should provide a summary of the key points and learning outcomes. The use of the handout should be flagged up at the beginning of the lecture during the contextual phase. Then the lecturer should navigate in a logical sequence through the handout, using it at appropriate moments to vary the stimulus and providing a thoughtful and stimulating activity.

Individual or group activities with interactive handouts

Interactive handouts provide activity and stimulation for individual students but encouraging students to work together in buzz groups can increase the level of interactivity. In a large lecture students can be asked to work together in twos and threes and even in eights with appropriate guidance. If there are gaps, questions or definitions to be inserted students can be given a few minutes to work together to come up with an answer. Students who have worked in this way are more open to further interactivity and will more easily respond to questions from the lecturer. In many ways the imaginative use of interactive handouts in lectures, coupled to student group activity, can achieve some of the deep learning benefits of small group teaching.

The quality of handouts

The ready availability of good quality printers and photocopiers means that handouts should be of the highest standard. They should be clear, readable, attractive and stimulating. They should be well structured and organized, with appropriate headings, and should contain sufficient space for students to insert material if required. The language of the handout should be simple and concise and aimed at a suitable level of understanding. Images and diagrams should be clear and unambiguous. Handouts should not be photocopies of photocopies of photocopies where the text is starting to disintegrate and the images are losing their contrast. Handouts should be regularly updated and printed out in appropriate batches each year.

This is always important but may be crucial for partially sighted students in your lectures. When preparing handout materials for students with a disability, it may be useful to refer to recent guidance (SWANDS, 2002) which recommends the following in appropriate circumstances:

- Provide materials in advance and electronically so that students can access them in a preferred format ahead of the lecture.
- Design materials with clarity firmly in mind using a sans serif font, such as Arial, in a font size of 12+, with text broken up with white space and avoiding excessive capitalization.
- Provide handouts on buff or pale coloured paper rather than white.
- Provide brief glossaries of important terms which can be very helpful to dyslexic students.

When to hand out handouts

Depending on their use, handouts can be given out at the beginning of a lecture, during the lecture or at the end. Alternatively, they can be provided online for students to print-off before the lecture. If the handouts are a summary of the key points of the lecture and are designed to minimize note taking then they should be given out at the beginning with appropriate instructions. If they contain additional material, reading lists or references then they can be given out at the end. If the handouts are of the interactive variety then they can be given out at the beginning or at an appropriate moment during the lecture, bearing in mind the slight disruption caused by their distribution. An interactive handout that is closely integrated with the content and sequence of the lecture should clearly be given out at the beginning.

Whenever they are given out there should be clear instructions on their use and the lecturer should monitor that they are being used correctly. It is worthwhile asking students not to start reading through the handout and to pay attention to the lecturer. If copies of overheads are provided in the handouts then students should be asked just to look at the overhead image being displayed and annotate it rather than reading forward and possibly losing the thread of an argument.

CASE STUDY: RS15 – OUTLINE OF AN 'ACTIVE' LECTURE

'RS15' is the fifteenth lecture in a series of lectures on the respiratory system for a mixed class of first-year medical students and pharmacists. The delivery of the lecture is closely linked to the two-page interactive handout shown in Figures 7.1 and 7.2. During the lecture there is a mixture of presentation, explanation, questioning and student activity. Not only does this lecture demonstrate the use of an interactive handout in an active lecture; it also shows how prior factual knowledge is activated and how students are encouraged to apply their knowledge and solve problems.

- The lecturer begins by welcoming the mixed group of students and pointing out a photograph of a man in an intensive care unit with broken ribs who is suffering from respiratory failure. This acts as a focus and context for the importance and relevance of the lecture. The lecturer introduces the interactive handout, which was picked up as the students entered the lecture theatre, and prepares them to involve themselves in the activities to come. The lecturer revises and activates previous knowledge by working through key information using an overhead image of Figure 7.1.

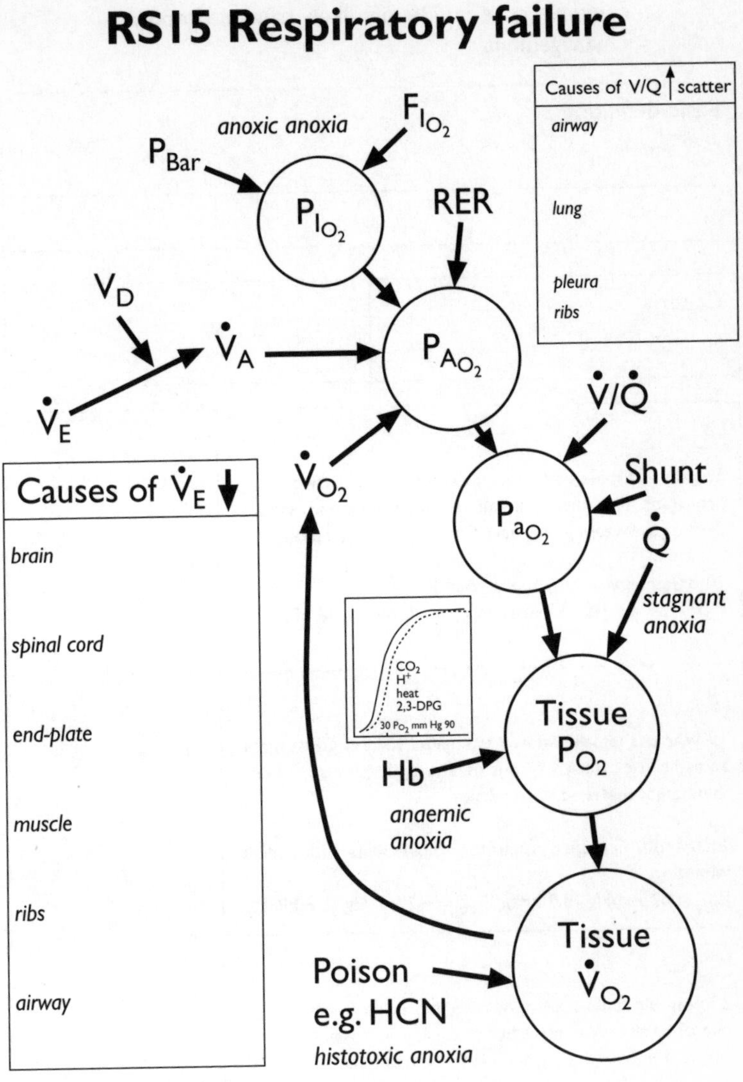

FIGURE 7.1 An interactive handout used for the lecture on respiratory failure (I)

RS15

Objective: Construct a definition of respiratory failure and devise suitable criteria; identify likely causes; propose management.

Basic definition

Criteria	

A 57 year old male with severe exacerbation of chronic bronchitis, brought to casualty by ambulance with severe dyspnoea, sweating and deeply reddish-purple colour. 20 breaths/min, many moist sounds P_{aO_2} = 50 mmHg (6.7 kPa), P_{aCO_2} = 60 mmHg (8 kPa)	
B 19 year old female, known asthmatic, seen in GP surgery an asthmatic attack which is persisting despite using her salbutamol metered dose inhaler. 11 breaths/min, deep respiratory movements with audible wheezing. P_{aO_2} = 67 mmHg (8.9 kPa), P_{aCO_2} = 42 mmHg (5.6 kPa)	
C 37 year old male building worker has fallen 6 feet onto a pile of bricks. Was brought to casualty in a workmate's car, and unconscious when removed from car. 24 breath/min, paradoxical movements of right side of chest. Pale and sweating; blueish lips P_{aO_2} = 45 mmHg (6 kPa), P_{aCO_2} = 45 mmHg (6 kPa)	

FIGURE 7.2 An interactive handout used for the lecture on respiratory failure (II)

- At twelve minutes the lecturer initiates a student activity by asking them to discuss, in a buzz group for two minutes, factors that might cause a fall in ventilation rate. This information is to be listed in the table on the left of the handout on Figure 7.1. After the buzz group answers are elicited by asking students to raise their hands if they have written down certain information. This activity takes about ten minutes. The lecturer then describes and discusses the information needed for students to fill in the upper table in Figure 7.1.
- At twenty-five minutes further explanation leads to a definition of respiratory failure and the filling in of the 'Basic definition' box in Figure 7.2.
- Students are next encouraged to think about particular levels of oxygen and carbon dioxide that define Type I and Type II respiratory failure. Using a 'voting' system the lecturer gets students to put up their hands for particular values that are discussed, evaluated and then used to fill in the 'criteria' boxes.
- At thirty-three minutes students are again asked to work in buzz groups to look at the three case vignettes. They have to decide whether each is a case of Type I or Type II respiratory failure.
- At thirty-six minutes student responses are elicited by a show of hands and the results discussed, evaluated and inserted into the appropriate boxes.
- At forty minutes the lecturer informs the students that there will be five minutes for questions before summarizing.
- At forty-six minutes the lecturer summarizes the key points of the lecture.

IN SUMMARY

Handouts are an important adjunct to contemporary lecturing practice. They have a wide range of styles and uses and if designed correctly and used appropriately can enhance the quality of learning.

FURTHER READING

Chin, P. (2004) *Using C&IT to Support Teaching*. London: RoutledgeFalmer.

SWANDS (South West Academic Network for Disability Support) (2002) 'Preparing documents', in *SENDA Compliance in HE*, SWANDS Project, University of Plymouth. http://www.plym.ac.uk/pages/view.asp?page=3243

USEFUL WEB SITES

http://www.cshe.unimelb.edu.au/downloads/revised_handouts/prep_lecture_notes_rev2.doc. James, R. (n.d.) *Preparing Lecture Notes and Handouts*.

Chapter 8

Computing and information technology in lecturing

INTRODUCTION

What will lectures look and feel like in ten or twenty years' time? How are teachers and university planners preparing to harness and integrate developments in technology? What facilities will a modern lecture theatre have and how will the students be asked to work and learn in the lectures of tomorrow?

This chapter attempts to crystal ball gaze and consult with the innovators of today to predict some of the future. The lecture methods and approaches discussed here are being developed, piloted and implemented by motivated and informed enthusiasts – the challenge will be for their work to be adopted and transferred to the mainstream. It is interesting to note some relatively recent C&IT developments that have done just that, and appreciate the drivers that have enabled that to happen. For example, can we imagine life without email, can we remember what it was like before we were encouraged to post our course outlines, lecture notes or reading lists onto Blackboard or WebCT, can we remember when we saw our first animated PowerPoint presentation? Many such insertions of technological teaching support are currently being integrated into our collective practice. What is next?

It is impossible to be comprehensive so this chapter will focus on a few areas of growing interest that include:

- using handsets for interactive lecturing
- consulting internet resources and information in the lecture
- live links and discussions using video conferencing
- using virtual learning environments (VLEs) to support the lecture.

USING HANDSETS FOR INTERACTIVE LECTURING

The arguments for the use of interactive approaches in lectures have been made in Chapter 6. In summary these are:

- to 'engage' and interest students so motivating them to learn
- to help students learn better – improve results
- to help students identify and build upon what they know already
- to help students check and review their understanding
- to give the lecturer feedback on student understanding (and their own teaching) etc.

Dr Steve Draper, Department of Psychology, University of Glasgow finds that using interactive handsets supports his lectures in three ways:

- Having a few very simple questions, to check understanding, after each chunk of talking reassures the students they have followed the main points, or tells them which point they should look at again. It seems to give the lecture a feeling of closure for them; and also of community (seeing whether they all got it right, or that quite a lot had trouble; tells them whether and how to talk to each other about it).

- Responses to questions can be used to steer what you say next (if they all get it right, speed onwards; if many have trouble, re-explain in more detail). This is obviously a good idea in a revision lecture; but we should probably use this more often to focus the lecture on where the difficulties lie.

- Handsets can be useful to get discussion going e.g. set a brain teaser, get them to vote, don't state the answer, require them to discuss with their neighbours which answers seem best to them. Active discussion is far more inducive of learning than passive listening.

How do interactive handsets work?

The lecturer displays a multiple-choice question using an OHP or projected PowerPoint. The students each select an answer from a range of possible alternatives and then submit their answers using their own push-button handset. After a minute or so the software projects the collective class results and shows a graph of how many students selected each of the possible answers. The lecturer can then use and respond to the class views in a variety of ways depending on the original learning outcomes for the session. The lecturer may comment on the range of answers that the students have given, or use the different opinions to trigger a whole-class discussion or to instigate conversations between pairs of students. Alternatively he or she may tell the students the correct answer and move on to the next section of the lecture.

The handsets and the equipment needed

The handsets look like TV remote controls and are distributed one per student (or possibly one per group). The handsets send an infrared signal to a receiver that in turn is linked, by cables, to a PC laptop. The laptop computer has software installed that allows quick analysis of the handset signals and collates and displays the results graphically via a data projector. When all wired together this set-up can be referred to as a Classroom Communication System (CCS).

There are several handset systems now commercially available, for example EduCue distributes the Personal Response System (PRS). See **Using PRS EduCue in Genetics**, in the 'Examples from different disciplines', section of this chapter (see pages 127–30) for more about the use of this system.

Distribution and allocation of the handsets to students can be managed in a number of different ways. They can be given out in the class by a group of nominated student helpers, they can be allocated to students for the whole period of study, or students can be required to buy handsets, which are then bought back by the university when they finish their course.

Making use of the handset technology

The ability of the handset technology to get a quick, individualized response from a large class of students has several practical advantages.

It is easy for students to use and allows them effectively to vote anonymously. The students benefit from seeing how their responses compare with the rest of the class and the lecturer gets instant feedback about how the students are thinking, understanding, feeling, etc. Lecturers can use student responses to inform and guide their inputs, for example: 'Quite a few people got that wrong so I need to explain it again in a different way.' The lecturer can also use the public generation of different points of view to initiate debate and discussion. In subjects where the concept of the 'right answer' can be a misnomer but the importance of a justified argument is central, the technology can be used to ask students to defend their point of view.

A common approach is to use the system to coordinate a live quiz or multiple choice styled test (MCQ) for the class. The quiz questions can:

- test the degree of initial understanding of a topic, to allow the lecturer to do on-the-spot adaptation of the lecture to suit the needs of the students better
- test the degree of understanding at the end of the session to allow self-assessment of how well understanding was achieved
- trigger and seed small group discussions, by posing questions that will result in a spread of responses and then asking students to discuss and defend their position with their peers
- provide feedback to lecturers on several dimensions of their lecture, i.e. the content, the teaching process, the skills of the lecturer, etc.

Nicol and Boyle (2003) have recently compared two methods of sequencing discussion using the handset 'voting' response mechanism. Method one involves answering a question and voting individually before going on to discuss the responses with a small group of peers. This sequence has been referred to as 'peer instruction' (Mazur 1997). The second method asks students to discuss their views in small groups before they individually respond to a question and this process has been called 'class-wide discussion' (Dufresne *et al.* 1996). Table 8.1 provides a comparison of the sequence of activities experienced in both the peer instruction and class-wide discussion methods.

Although both processes have been shown to aid learning, Nicol and Boyd's work has indicated that peer instruction was perceived by their students to be more beneficial to learning than the class-wide discus-

TABLE 8.1 The sequence of activities in peer instruction and class-wide discussion

Peer instruction: Mazur sequence	Class-wide discussion: Dufresne sequence
1. Concept question posed 2. *Individual thinking*: students given time to think individually (1–2 minutes) 3. Students provide individual responses 4. Students receive feedback – poll of responses presented as histogram display 5. *Peer discussion*: students instructed to convince their neighbours that they have the right answer. 6. Retesting of same concept 7. Students provide individual responses (revised answer) 8. Students receive feedback – poll of responses presented as histogram display 9. Lecturer summarizes and explains 'correct' response	1. Concept question posed 2. *Peer discussion*: small groups discuss the concept question (3–5 mins) 3. Students provide individual or group responses 4. Students receive feedback – poll of responses presented as histogram display. *Class-wide discussion*: students explain their answers and listen to the explanations of others (facilitated by tutor) 5. Lecturer summarizes and explains 'correct' response

Source: Nicol and Boyle 2003

sion sequencing. Teaching staff also found the peer instruction format to be easier to organize and manage in the larger lectures. Intuitively this seems logical. Asking students to think about and answer a question for themselves gives space for all the students to engage in the process and lessens the likelihood that conversations will be dominated by a few. The discussions should be richer and draw upon a more diverse range of views with students having had the time to develop their own positions before being influenced by the thinking of others.

CONSULTING INTERNET RESOURCES AND INFORMATION

Lecturers can now access the world in the lecture theatre and the potential use of the Internet and electronic links may in the future be limited only by our imaginations.

Using web-based information sources in the lecture theatre can demonstrate to students how they can carry out their own further research. It also provides the opportunity to discuss the evaluation of web-based sources and to introduce the students to the wide range of information they can readily find on the Internet.

> OK, now let's have a look at the latest guidelines from the Department of Health on treating asthma in the under-fives.
>
> If we look at the manufacturer's specified range for this product and compare it with the range we see being used in our case study – we may begin to see some reasons for the detected inefficiency? Let's have a look at the latest published information – as we can see, this page was updated only last week so this is the current information being provided by the makers . . .

In practice it may well be worth cheating! Trying to access the Internet live in front of 150 students may be a little risky. The server may choose that moment to crash, or the site you are looking for may be being maintained and is unavailable, and so on. Lecturers can avoid these headaches by downloading information or copying the web pages onto their laptop computer just before the lecture.

LIVE PEOPLE LINKS AND DISCUSSIONS

The technology now means that it is possible to ask scientists in the arctic about their work or consult an expert in the British Museum during the lecture. This is fantastically exciting and live interactions make a super addition to a lecture. The technology still falls over with reasonable frequency and therefore it is unwise to rely on it totally. Experienced teachers always have a low-tech backup strategy up their sleeve.

Video conferencing is being used in response to some of the difficulties created by the Widening Participation agenda and general expansion in HE and FE. Increasing class sizes may require split-site delivery of some lectures; speciality courses may need to be shared between universities because of the lack of teachers with the necessary knowledge and skills; HE-level lecture courses may be transmitted to students in FE colleges, etc.

There are two common ways in which video conferencing is being used for lecturing. The first is to deliver a whole lecture course to

FIGURE 8.1 'Beaming in from the beach'

students who are in two locations: a home site (with the lecturer) and a remote site (which might be next door or overseas). The second method is to have special event 'keynote' lectures within a course using video conferencing. Here the idea is to invite specialists or experts to contribute to a course and so give the benefit of their insight and background in a topic without the need for them to come to the students.

In evaluating these different options Pitcher *et al*. (2000) noted that lecturers felt that video conferencing could be used successfully to 'lecture at a distance' but that a different style and lecture format may be needed. For example, students at a remote site will only be able to see what appears on their monitor. It is therefore very important that the visual stimulus transmitted via the monitor is varied and carefully linked to the oral message that they hear from the lecturer. So the lecture may need to be more carefully organized and choreographed. The 'distant' students also felt that it was very important to be able to see the lecturer's face regularly throughout the lecture in order to maintain the human communication process. The lecturers also felt that the students 'at a distance' needed to be engaged in the lecture much more explicitly and they commented on the need to include icebreakers and question and answer sessions to maintain the link with the students.

Student reactions to the different forms of video conferencing were also interesting. When a whole lecture course was conveyed using video conferencing the majority of students were either mildly unenthusiastic or neutral about the teaching method; whereas the 'keynote' special lecture was very positively evaluated. Many students admitted that they found it more difficult to concentrate in a video conferencing lecture and they didn't feel that they had learnt any more in this way (compared with a traditionally delivered lecture). However when Pitcher *et al*. compared the assessment results between the home and distant students in a video conferencing study they found that the remote students had not been negatively affected.

Carville and Mitchell (2000) felt the main disadvantage of using a video conferencing system between Belfast (home site) and Armagh (the remote site), when teaching early childhood studies, was a lack of interactivity. They observed that the interactivity between the students in the two sites and between the teacher and the students was significantly reduced. It will be very worthwhile exploring ways of overcoming these concerns, as the benefits of video conferencing are clear. For example, the use of the technology in this case has widened access to training and education for students who are working professionals living in rural areas of Northern Ireland and the college is investing and expanding its video conferencing provision for the future.

For many, however, it maybe more realistic to envisage exchanges and discussions happening asynchronously, after the lecture, for example asking students to follow up issues raised in the lecture via a discussion forum, situated within a virtual learning environment (VLE). A growing number of course leaders are investing their energies in developing VLEs that include a range of course support mechanisms, information and resources. By dovetailing the virtual world of a VLE with the live provision of a lecture the teacher can potentially provide a more flexible mode of study. For example, if the large number of students in the class inhibits even the bravest from asking a question at the end, replace that part of the lecture with a virtual directed discussion or include an FAQs (frequently asked questions) section on the VLE for students to review afterwards.

USING VLEs TO SUPPORT THE LECTURE

The current use of Virtual Learning Environments (VLEs), such as Blackboard or WebCT, has very much focused on three areas of course provision. First, course management and administration: providing reading lists, class registers, timetables, contact details, etc. Second, their potential in supporting small group teaching activities is being widely explored by asking students to take part in virtual seminars and online discussions, and visit topic-based chat rooms (Exley and Dennick 2004). Third, as a place to provide the students with additional learning resources whether they be useful web links, downloadable articles, lecture notes, PowerPoint files or self-testing quizzes etc.

The use of VLEs to support large group teaching, and in particular the lecture, is probably less well explored, although the replacement of lectures with interactive learning tasks provided through the VLE is a growing trend. Here our clear focus is the support of the lecture itself.

VLEs can provide a significant support for learning in a lecture-based course by stimulating students to prepare for their lectures and then to reflect upon and review their learning after the lecture.

Taking a constructivist approach to how our students are learning places a great emphasis on the students being able to build on their prior knowledge and experience (see series website guide, Brown 2004). A pre-lecture task, therefore, may invite the students to work through a multiple choice test or respond to a set of open questions in order to refresh and, if you like, 'turn the soil' of their previous exposure to the lecture topic. What do they know or believe already? What questions do they have about the topic? How does the new lecture topic link with other parts of the course i.e. activate prior learning?

Providing a small set of required readings linked to the outcomes of a self-testing quiz can help the students clarify their own learning outcomes for lectures. If the students know why they are attending a lecture and what they personally want to get out of it there can be a greater level of active participation and involvement in the class.

The same approach used partway through a lecture course can give the students the chance to see if they are indeed understanding and internalizing the material and concepts covered in the lectures. Students can be organized into 'study groups' and asked to meet after lectures to complete phase test questions. Alternatively, the phase test can be part of the continuous assessment for a course and the students can be asked to work independently (in a supervised room). Through both these approaches the lecturer gets feedback on the levels of student understanding and can respond and adapt future lectures in the latter half of the course.

VLEs can also provide opportunities for students and lecturers to talk to each other using a discussion forum after the lectures. Students can ask questions and clarify points or further explore an area and follow up on suggested readings.

In my ecology and conservation course I used online conferencing to reflect on lecture sessions by posing questions immediately after a lecture and to support students, leading up to the examinations, with responses to individual queries for all to see, etc.

(Susan Barker, University of Warwick)

A word about technical back-up and expertise

We are gradually moving into a world in which universities and colleges are employing technical assistants to support well-resourced lecture theatres – teaching environments in which lecturers are not expected to sort out all the equipment for themselves and to become an expert in the necessary software and hardware they need to embrace some of the exciting developments that technology can bring. However, the provision and level of support is very variable from one institution to the next and indeed from one department to the next. Finding out what your institution does provide in the way of technical support is important. It is very hard work to be a trailblazer with technology and finding supportive and interested colleagues to discuss and innovate with is enormously beneficial.

EXAMPLES FROM DIFFERENT DISCIPLINES

Mechanical engineering

Concerns about teaching and learning that led to the use of interactive handsets in large lectures

In 1998 the 'New Approaches to Teaching and Learning in Engineering' (NATALIE) initiative was launched at the University of Strathclyde. The aim was to revitalize teaching and learning in the undergraduate degree programme of the Department of Mechanical Engineering. Three areas of concern led to this initiative.

Firstly, lecturers had noticed that most first year students had difficulty acquiring a deep understanding of certain core concepts. As one lecturer put it 'even the brightest students make inexplicable blunders in the application of these concepts' . . . They usually occur when the concept conflicts with intuitive beliefs and/or when the concept is highly complex, involving multiple, and often interacting, components.

A second concern was the increasing numbers in lecture classes that limited the potential for interaction and discussion. Lecturers complained that because the flow of information was mainly one-way it was difficult to identify when students were experiencing difficulties.

A third area of concern was the motivation of the students. Some lecturers argued that new technology and the information rich society had undermined the value of lectures. Nowadays, students preferred to concentrate for short intense periods on a task or to multi-task rather than to concentrate for long periods of time in lectures.

(Boyle and Nicol 2003)

Using PRS EduCue in Genetics

I've very recently become a convert to using a Personal Response System to do interactive Q & As in my lectures. The system consists of infrared student handsets communicating to the PowerPoint questions embedded in my lecture. I first saw it demonstrated at an American conference and realized that for £4000 I could purchase 95 handsets, IR detector, the software and a dedicated laptop to interact with my undergraduate classes. At the time the system had not hit the UK so with a grant from my University's teaching enhancement scheme I bought a set from the USA. Now this was probably madness, as I am known as not being very computer literate by my colleagues. Luckily I was saved in setting up the system by two wonderful technocrat colleagues. We did have significant teething troubles with the US software that we were originally sent, but this was then replaced with RXShow software from a different company and we were able to roll! RXShow happily includes several template slides from which a technophobe like me was able to construct my own simply by pasting and manipulating in PowerPoint. I was able to paste in figures and questions and to test knowledge as well as opinions and ideas.

So how does it work? Well, firstly you set up your laptop or computer connected to the data projector and connected via a USB port to the infrared detector which you Blu-Tack™ to the front of the lecture theatre above head height (just above our theatre whiteboard works!). Next, the students each collect their numbered responder handset (these can be specifically assigned or given out at random). I have found it very helpful to buy the proper carry-cases for the responders, in which the handsets are set out in numbered ranks, as it really helps a large class of students to quickly pick up specific units.

The first slide in the interactive part of the presentation is a 'register' showing all the numbers of units in the class as individual 'tiles'. The students each log in by pressing '1' and their numbered tile changes colour when the receiver has picked up their signal. This can double as the register for the class where students are always assigned the same number unit. A few minutes are required for this stage as there will always be a couple of students in a large class who have a unit with a flat battery or are pointing it the wrong way! Good news is the battery life is long and they're rechargeable. Also, even in a 200-seat lecture theatre there is good strength of signal to reach a single receiver at the front (except when pointed through someone else's head!). You can then proceed with ordinary PowerPoint slides or directly to your first question slide. The options for questions are true/false/abstain or multiple choice (with up to nine options, but I use five max). The students respond using their units and a rolling tally box on the slide records the advancing percentage of respondents. One drawback of a large lecture theatre is that this rarely reaches 100 per cent but all students will feel they have contributed after about one minute of pressing buttons. Clicking to the next slide then pops up a histogram or pie chart (your choice of several designs) showing the percentage responses to each option. You and they can see the split of the vote and you can go through which answer was right. (Wits in the audience who have not previously voted can enjoy pressing buttons to raise the percentage of the last answer as the lecturer advances through all the prior choices as being false!).

Other slide formats allow you to click up to half a dozen specified numbered responders only and to ask just those students to answer a question (a bit intimidating!). Another format lets students volunteer to answer a particular question by clicking '1' to volunteer. Neither of these was very popular with the 95 second-year undergraduates with whom I've piloted the system. However, when asked (by PRS) how many thought the handsets would be useful, or very useful, to aid understanding (used anonymously in lectures without responder numbers being assigned), 83 per cent said yes, 15 per cent were neutral and 2 per cent said no.

I'm realizing that the system has loads of uses including Week 1 registration meetings with shy freshers (trying to gauge what they really have learned in school) and at academic staff meetings! I'm going to try it in all my undergraduate modules next year (I have a trolley to tote the cases to the lecture hall). The students suggest it is used in a ten-minute session as the end of each topic block (every three lectures or so) to test their knowledge . . . I'm going to see when fatigue sets in or if any of the units disappear (not that they can be used as a TV remote as I have made a point of explaining!).

I like the system and its relative affordability and portability. I'm going to use it in a field station this summer at an evening round-up after a day's experimenting. Its real advantage is that it can draw out all in a class, even the most shy, to tell you what they think the answer to your questions is. This is great as you can really see 'if they get it' before moving on to build their knowledge further. The only drawback I've found so far is that without the registering tile showing on each slide students can't tell each time if their vote has been registered (just the total percentage who have voted shows in a box); however, if they keep pressing they will get through! I'm currently recommending PRS to all my friends.

(Dr Liz Sockett, Genetics, University of Nottingham, personal communication)

Using video conferencing – an interactive keynote lecture in medicine

This lecture involved the transmission of live video from an audio-visual studio to a group of forty clinical medical students in a lecture theatre. The image was projected on to a large screen and sound was provided from the speaker output of two monitors at the front of the lecture theatre. The lecturer in the studio was provided with a monitor showing a wide view of the whole lecture theatre from a camera on the front bench and sound input from the audience from one hand-held radio microphone. The lecturer was in charge of the images shown to the students. By pressing an appropriate button he could transmit either images of himself, slides, overheads or patients he was interviewing and examining. The lecturer talked to the audience, showed slides and interviewed patients. In addition the lecturer asked the audience questions and received responses from them via a hand-held microphone distributed by an audio-visual technician.

There was a brief presentation on a clinical topic, 'ulcerative colitis', during which the lecturer talked through images and text slides in the conventional way, explaining technical issues with the aid of clear diagrams. At a number of points during the presentation the lecturer asked the students questions and they were able to respond using the hand-held microphone, which they passed amongst them.

The lecturer next turned to talking to a patient, taking a history and performing an examination. Students were able to follow this procedure and were again asked to respond to the lecturer's questions.

The patient was thanked for her cooperation and left the studio. The final section of the lecture then involved the lecturer asking a series of searching and challenging questions to the students, encouraging them to apply and use their developing clinical knowledge to discuss possible diagnoses, further investigations and management plans.

Observation of the students indicated they were engaging with the presentation, taking notes and concentrating in the normal manner. The actual structure of the presentation was well organized with a variety of stimuli ranging from direct talking to camera, talking over slides with a pointer and talking to and listening to patients. The lecture was long (1.5 hours) and covered a large amount of material; nevertheless the lecturer controlled and organized the presentation in a lively and stimulating way.

This technique enabled the doctor to work with a patient in the large group teaching session, as the patient did not find it intimidating being in the studio and could feel more at ease and behave naturally. A good lecturer, trained in the technique, can provide a well organized and stimulating lecture to a group of students at a remote site. Interactivity can occur and questioning can become a regular feature of such presentations. The learning occurring during such a lecture is not impaired in comparison to a normal live lecture. In fact it is possible that there is an enhancement of learning due to the very large image and the high quality sound and that questioning and interactivity enable the lecturer to ask challenging and thought provoking questions. There is a certain irony that this can occur more easily using a video link in comparison to a conventional lecture.

(Lecturer in medical education)

FURTHER READING

Exley, K. and Dennick, R. (2004) 'Using C&IT in small group teaching', in *Small Group Teaching*. London: RoutledgeFalmer.

Laurillard, D. (1993) *Rethinking University Teaching: A Framework for the Effective Use of Educational Technology*. London: RoutledgeFalmer.

USEFUL WEB SITES

Brown, G. (2004) *How Students Learn*. http://routledgefalmer.com/series/KGETHE

http://www.bedu.com/Publications/physlectAPF.html Parlis, J. and Massen, C. (1997) *Physics Lecturing with Audience Paced Feedback*.

http://www.psy.gla.ac.uk/~steve/ilig/local.html#intro) Draper, S. (2003) *Using Handsets at Glasgow University*.

Chapter 9

Student diversity

INTRODUCTION

In a large lecture the lecturer may initially see the student audience as a sea of faces. However, it usually doesn't take long before you spot people you recognize and the faceless crowd gradually transforms into a group of individuals who have very different needs, concerns and interests. Trying to design and deliver lectures with this diversity in mind is important. You clearly can't appeal to all the students all the time but by varying your approach and the stimulus you can reach more of the people in the room.

There are some students in every cohort who have more specific learning needs and this chapter seeks to provide a gateway to thinking about supporting them in the lecture theatre.

The needs of students who have a disability such as a visual impairment, a hearing problem, or who are dyslexic, are considered in more detail here, as these are perhaps the most frequently occurring disabilities in the student population. However, the 'Further reading' section of this chapter does provide links to information sources that can offer guidance on the support of students who have a wider range of disabilities and difficulties.

International students, who are non-native speakers of English, may also need your particular consideration in the lecture and we will briefly outline some simple measures that a teacher can take to help overseas students in the lecture.

The final group of students we will consider are those who have less confidence in the lecture. This may be because they are returning to their studies as mature students and have had time away from formal education. It may also include students who are entering higher education from a further education course in which the student numbers in individual classes were much lower and there was a greater emphasis on the taught curriculum, with relative contact hours with teaching staff being much higher.

STUDENTS WHO HAVE A DISABILITY

College- and university-level support

In response to recent legislation (Special Educational Needs Disability Act, 2002) all educational institutions in the UK have reviewed and significantly enhanced their procedural and policy support for their students who have disabilities. (See Appendix 1 for a quick review of the legal position with regard to the support of students who have a disability.)

Written guidelines and codes of practice are now commonplace. However, the UK is certainly not alone in responding to the needs of a growing and diverse student body. For example, Table 9.1 shows The Code of Practice in relation to lecturing produced in 1991 by the University of New South Wales, Australia (UNSW).

When seeking to support students who have a disability there are two general approaches:

- **Compensatory strategies**: working around the areas of deficit or loss and using strengths to acquire new knowledge, understanding and skills (i.e. taped lecture notes for partially sighted students, or the use of colour coding to help students with hearing/processing difficulties).
- **Learning strategies**: teaching how to learn, helping the students to enhance or develop their strategies for time management and how to listen, read and take notes effectively and, very importantly, to learn appropriate revision and examination skills.

Individual needs

If you are aware that any students in your lecture have a disability try to arrange to speak with them, privately, to discuss their needs at the earliest opportunity. Try not to make global assumptions about their

TABLE 9.1 The required response and strategies outlined in the Code of Practice – Students with Disabilities, UNSW

Strategies

- Lecturers should, in consultation with the student and relevant authorities, be free to vary the methods of presentation of work and or assessment, in order to accommodate the nature of the particular disability, providing that academic standards are not compromised.
- Academic staff shall allow students with a disability to use specialized equipment particular to the disability required for that student's participation in lectures, tutorials or laboratory situations.
- Wherever possible, and in co-operation with lecturers, lectures and tutorials will be re-located, if scheduled in a location which creates access difficulties in getting to a lecture between lectures and tutorials.
- With co-operation of lecturers concerned, students with disabilities may tape record for purposes of their study, lecture, tutorial or laboratory material.
- Lecturers should provide copies of their lecture notes and/or overhead projector transparencies if necessary, to students with disabilities for study purposes.
- Lecturers should be encouraged to provide Reading Lists and course related material to students with visual, hearing or physical disabilities, prior to the commencement of academic sessions as these students often need to have material put into different media, e.g. FM Receivers, sign interpreters.
- Academic staff should be provided with the opportunities to be trained in the appreciation of specialized items of equipment being used by students with disabilities, e.g. FM Receivers, sign interpreters.
- An Academic staff member shall be nominated by each School to act as a Contact Person for students with disabilities within that school. Students with disabilities however, should have the freedom to approach other members of staff if they prefer.

disability; the students will be the experts on their own condition and situation. Discuss their needs with them in order to understand their position better and ask for their advice on how you can support their learning and help them to participate fully in your class (Exley and Dennick 2004).

If you would like to find out more about a particular kind of disability or better understand a particular disabling condition, there is a list of information websites, which you may find useful, at the end of this book (Appendix 2).

Helping students who have a visual impairment

The handout material provided by many teachers in a lecture will need to be adapted for use by students with sight difficulties. Depending on the severity of their disability and preferred learning style, students may wish to use material in braille or large print format, or even be provided with notes on audio-tape. Some students may be provided with the support of specially trained 'readers' who will read aloud lecture handout materials for them before the lecture. This is clearly time-consuming so it is very important that the students be provided

FIGURE 9.1 'The advance of technology'
'I drew the line when two students walked into my lecture, placed taperecorders on the first row, set them going and then left.'

with any handout material well ahead of the lecture. Obtaining reading lists at short notice also creates problems for these students. Reading enlarged print on buff-coloured paper or using computer-based, print magnification equipment is also more time-consuming and tiring.

Some students will ask if they can bring a tape recorder to your lecture. This has been a controversial request in some universities. Teachers have voiced fears that an audio-record of their lectures may misrepresent their 'live' lecture, and there are concerns about issues of copyright and future litigation. There are also problems for students who rely on tape transcriptions. Listening to tapes as a method of learning requires sophisticated listening and abstraction skills and high levels of concentration. Above all it is more time-consuming than ordinary reading. However, despite these problems the presence of several tape recorders in lectures is now becoming more commonplace.

Using visual aids in the lecture is strongly recommended and provides an important support for the learning of the majority of students in the lecture. However, lecturers will need to take the time to explain images and visuals used in the lecture for the benefit of their partially sighted students. Alternatively, some students may wish to be provided with copies of the visual aids displayed in a format that they can more readily interact with before or during the class (e.g. large, black and white images in a handout, or copies that can be accessed on the intranet and viewed using magnification equipment). Negotiation with the students about the formats and approach that best suit their individual needs is clearly important.

Helping students with a hearing impairment in your lecture

Students with hearing impairment are frequently disadvantaged in a university situation as most lectures, seminars and tutorials are oral. The poor acoustics and lighting in many old-fashioned lecture theatres and the lack of adequate sound systems all contribute to their difficulties. Some students must rely on a direct microphone link to the lecturer to hear the lecture but this does mean that they won't be able to hear questions raised by other students.

Universities are, no doubt, slowly updating their teaching accommodation and facilities and are placing a greater emphasis on the design of new teaching rooms and taking care about the choice of equipment installed to provide more support for students with hearing difficulties. This is, however, a costly and therefore an incremental process, which in the shorter term means that many lecturers are asked to teach in less than ideal circumstances.

Background noise can be very distracting and troubling for students who are wearing hearing aids. The lecturer, if aware of this, can make sure that this is kept to a minimum. Many students will also use lip reading extensively to follow the lecture. The obvious, but very easily forgotten, need is to keep facing them as you talk. Make sure these students sit near and in a place in the lecture theatre that you naturally face when lecturing.

Some deaf students may use the services of people employed by the college or university to help them, such as signers, realtime captionists or note takers. The lecturer clearly needs to coordinate activities with them.

A realtime captionist is a stenographer who uses a steno-machine to take down a lecture verbatim just as in a Law Court. The words of the lecturer are made instantly available on the screen of a laptop computer. The deaf student is therefore able to read the lecture as it is presented. People and equipment need to be positioned so that the student can see the lecturer and the computer screen at the same time and so that the lecturer is not distracted during the class. This will require discussion and agreement. As there are likely to be technical or unusual words used in many lectures the captionist would need to have access to this terminology before the lecture in order to be accurate for the student. Therefore, the lecturer would need to provide appropriate vocabulary lists or textbooks and liaise with the captionist about seating arrangements in the lecture theatre.

The student can take a copy of the lecture for his or her private study at the end of the class. The concerns raised by many lecturers about students having recordings or verbatim copies of their lectures on computer can be partially addressed by discouraging the dissemination of these recordings or notes to other students (who can hear and take notes from the lecture themselves). In the United States it is reasonably common for universities to ask their students with disabilities to sign a standard letter of agreement if they wish to use the services of a captionist or audio-record lectures, and this practice may well gather momentum in the United Kingdom – see Table 9.2.

TABLE 9.2 An agreement statement produced by The Office for Students with Disabilities at The University of California, Los Angeles

I understand that as a student receiving realtime captioning service, I will receive verbatim transcripts from the Office for Students with Disabilities as an accommodation based on my documented disability. These transcripts are solely for my personal academic use, and I may not share them with any other student or use them for any other purpose other than as class study notes without consultation with the Office for Students with Disabilities and the expressed consent of the professor.

Source: http://www.saonet.ucla.edu/osd/docs/FacInfo/RTCinfo.htm

Using sign language

Visual transmission of information takes longer than auditory transmission and so the lecturer needs to coordinate his or her delivery with that of the signer. Remember:

- Speak steadily especially when using technical terms that need to be finger-spelled.
- Direct questions and remarks to the student, not the signer, although the interpreter may voice the student's responses and questions for the teacher.
- Additionally, the lecturer should attempt to ensure that other students don't interrupt or talk over each other as this causes problems for both the signer and the hearing-impaired student.

(Advice based upon Yoshinaga-Itano 2002)

Helping dyslexic students in your lecture

Students with dyslexia may have difficulties with the following learning activities: reading; remembering, organizing and expressing ideas in writing; spelling, grammar and punctuation; handwriting; note taking; time management; and concentration (Farmer *et al*. 2002). Many of these will have a direct impact on the student in a lecture. Similar kinds of problems can occur with mathematical calculation and this is know as dyscalcula. However, it is important to remember that extraordinary achievements are frequently made by people with learning disabilities. Albert Einstein, Leonardo da Vinci and Thomas Edison are just some prominent individuals who are now alleged to have had dyslexia. However, the condition has only recently been identified and it still often goes undiagnosed.

What is dyslexia?

The British Dyslexia Association describes dyslexia and its effect as follows:

- Dyslexia is caused by a difference in the part of the brain that deals with language. There is evidence gathered from brain imaging techniques that dyslexic people process information differently.
- Dyslexia tends to run in families. Dyslexia continues throughout life. Around 4 per cent of the population is severely dyslexic. A further 6 per cent have mild to moderate problems.
- Dyslexia occurs in people from all backgrounds and of all abilities, from people who cannot read or write to those with university degrees. Dyslexic people may have creative, artistic, practical skills. They can develop strategies to compensate for their areas of difficulty.
- Dyslexia is a puzzling mix of both difficulties and strengths. It varies in degree and from person to person.

Teaching strategies

There are many teaching approaches that can help to negate some of the reading, writing and memory problems faced by dyslexic students. The lecturer can:

- provide a course syllabus at the start of term outlining the content and sequence of the lectures
- at the start of the lecture, write new terms and key points on the board
- provide frequent mini-summaries during the lecture and provide links and summaries at appropriate points across the course as a whole
- illustrate abstract concepts with concrete examples and with personal experiences

- when feasible bring theory and practice together using hands-on demonstrations
- use both oral and visual stimuli, i.e. lots of visual aids such as charts and graphs
- provide booklists in good time to allow students to begin the reading early or to have texts put on tape
- provide handouts and study guides that direct the student to key points in their 'homework' or preparatory readings
- read aloud material that is shown on an overhead projector, board or PowerPoint
- keep oral instructions concise and summarize them with brief cue words or bullet point lists.

Assisting note taking and alternative approaches

Some students with dyslexia and other learning disabilities need to make use of alternative ways of recording their learning from a lecture because they cannot write quickly enough or assimilate, remember and organize the material while also listening to the lecturer.

Some colleges are employing 'student note takers' to accompany dyslexic students to lectures and produce a record for them. Others encourage the use of tape recording lectures and yet others require lecturers to make a full and complete set of lecture notes available to students electronically after the class.

Teaching techniques that facilitate students in exchanging and reviewing their lecture notes with each other either during or after the class can help students to improve their note-taking skills.

Probably the most common method of support is to provide students with incomplete handouts (see Chapter 7) which provide the students with an organized framework in which they can annotate and add a limited number of their own additional notes and comments.

(Many of the strategies above will also be of benefit for the other students in the lecture, particularly non-native speakers of English.)

HELPING NON-NATIVE ENGLISH SPEAKERS IN YOUR LECTURE

To be as clear as possible it is likely that tutors will need to speak more loudly, more slowly and in shorter sentences than they may otherwise do. Care also needs to be taken in the choice of language and terminology chosen. Trying to avoid colloquial terms, acronyms, abbreviations, or jargon again probably benefits all students but particularly non-native speakers. Tutors should try to organize and structure their explanations and explicitly signpost their position in that structure at regular intervals throughout the lecture.

When teachers refer to a particular person or an important source it is helpful if they write the names or details up on the board or flipchart. Alternatively tutors can provide such information in a brief handout that the students can refer to and annotate during class. The active learning and interactive teaching strategies discussed earlier (Chapters 6 and 7) which aim to give students 'comfortable' thinking time and opportunities to check their understanding and note taking with their peers are also particularly helpful for non-native speakers (Exley and Dennick 2004).

As described for dyslexic students, the provision of handout notes in class will remove the need for international students to try and write quickly and comprehensively in a second or third language. It will reduce the pressure they feel to 'get it down' and give them more time to think about it during the lecture.

HELPING STUDENTS WHO APPEAR UNDER-CONFIDENT IN THE LECTURE

The Widening Participation agenda has had a dramatic impact in many institutions on the make-up of the student body. Some universities and colleges have been very successful in attracting non-traditional learners back to further and higher study. Mature students (over the age of 21) may have had a number of years away from a classroom setting and may not be used to a packed lecture theatre with two hundred students sitting in it. Mature students may feel alienated and deprived of the opportunity to ask questions in such an environment.

Similarly a group of students who can feel very under-confident in the lecture theatre are students who have entered higher education through an access route or a foundation degree. These students will frequently have had, during their one or more years in a further education college, a more directly supported experience of learning. Frequently FE classes are smaller, large parts of the courses are directly taught, course work is submitted and marked several times during a unit of study and students enjoy a much more personal relationship with teachers and tutors. Suddenly to find themselves in a potentially more anonymous educational system, which makes much greater use of independent learning strategies, can be very daunting. The taught components of the course may well be lectures and on large, popular, first-year courses these can be very large events indeed. In business or computing numbers often rise above three hundred students in a lecture.

Although the background and previous experience of these two groups of students are very different, some of the difficulties they face in the lecture may be similar:

- understanding the role of the lecture in their learning
- finding the best way of working in the lecture
- finding the best way of recording that learning, e.g. making notes or annotating handout materials
- being able to check their understanding and ask questions.

Many universities and colleges do provide excellent support through study skills workshops and advice and clearly some of these questions and concerns can be addressed here. However, particularly when teaching first-year groups, the lecturer can provide explicit guidance on how he or she expects the students to work in the lecture, when to put pens down and listen, when to take down diagrams or notes, etc. Students do view the skills of note taking as being of central importance when studying at university.

> Students initially perceived (and subsequently confirmed in the light of actual experience) that university was primarily about analysing information followed by taking notes.
>
> (Blicharski 1999)

The guidance given to students during study skills courses about note taking may well mirror these offered by the University of Bradford: (http://www.bradford.ac.uk/acad/civeng/skills/lectures.htm#lets) (accessed 19/06/03)

- Listen for the main points and record these, together with any supporting evidence.
- Listen for cues from the lecturer such as 'The main point is . . . There are two issues involved', etc.
- Leave room in your notes to add things later.
- Review your notes as soon as possible after the lecture.
- Discuss with other students.

As a lecturer it is worth considering which of these we can actually support. We can certainly stress key points and enhance the verbal and visual cues we give to help students recognize important points. We can give semi-structured or partial handouts that guide the note-taking process and explicitly leave room for students to embellish and expand for themselves. We can also build in 'review' exercises to encourage students to do this for themselves.

Building in time for lecture note swaps and summarizing discussions can also help students to double check their record of the lecture and develop their skills. For example, leaving five minutes at the end of the lecture, asking the students to write down the three most important aspects considered in the class and telling their neighbour why they chose them, can help less confident students consolidate their learning and increase their belief that they are doing the right thing.

Mature students often greatly value the opportunity to ask the lecturer questions to clarify points or to gain further insights and detail about a topic. In large lectures spontaneous exchange is problematic and the lecturer can seek to organize learning activities that generate questions in class (see Chapter 6). Alternatively the course may be designed to enable further discussion of the topics raised in the lecture in related tutorial sessions. If this isn't the case the use of follow-up discussion boards on the course VLE can support such exchanges (see Chapter 8).

Students from FE backgrounds may lack the confidence of many mature students in asking questions in an open forum. They may also be less experienced or skilled in finding and evaluating learning sources in texts and journals in the library or on the internet. It is worth keeping this in mind when planning reading lists and suggested follow-up readings at the end of the lecture.

IN SUMMARY

Many of the adaptations to the lecture suggested in this chapter will benefit all the students attending but may make a significant difference to individuals who have specific difficulties. They may make the difference between students dropping out of the course and continuing successfully. Widening Participation (WP) is not just about getting more students through the doors and onto courses; the heart of the matter is retention and progression. These two very dry words are about welcoming and supporting a wide and diverse group of learners as they go through a demanding personal transition. Adaptations to teaching and learning approaches are clearly only part of the fundamental change to the sector which is needed for WP policies to be successfully implemented. This debate draws us beyond the scope of the volume but for further information do consult the HEFCE reports 01/37 and 03/15 (HEFCE 2001, 2003).

FURTHER READING

Quality and Standards in Higher Education, Students with Disabilities (1999) The Quality Assurance Agency for Higher Education (QAA). http://www.qaa.ac.uk/public/COP/COPswd/contents.htm

Doyle, C. and Robson, K. (2001) *Accessible Curricula: Good Practice For All*, Cardiff: University of Wales. http://www.uwic.ac.uk/ltsu/accessible.pdf

Hayton, A. and Paczuska, A. (eds) (2002) *Participation and Higher Education*. London: Kogan Page.

Waterfield, J. and West, B. (2002) *SENDA Compliance in Higher Education*. Plymouth: South West Academic Network for Disability Support (SWANDS).

USEFUL WEB SITES

http://www.dmu.ac.uk/services/student_services/slas/dyslexia/inform_staff.jsp?ComponentID=5757&SourcePageID=5755#1 De Montfort University web pages giving guidance to staff on supporting dyslexic students

www.drc-gb.org For general information on disabilities and disabilities legislation

http://www.plymouth.ac.uk/disability For advice on making the curriculum accessible to disabled students

Chapter 10

Evaluating lecturing

To become a good lecturer you need to assess yourself against some agreed standards, change your practice in response to the feedback you obtain and, by repeating this cycle, gradually improve your skills, increase your confidence and hopefully enjoy your teaching more. One well-recognized set of standards forms the basis of quality assurance mechanisms in higher education, used, for example, by the Quality Assurance Agency (Quality Assurance Agency 2003).

To a large extent they reflect the recommendations for lecturing we have described in previous chapters. This chapter will list the main criteria used during teaching evaluation as well as looking at some common presentational problems and their solutions. It will then describe some typical teaching evaluation techniques and describe how to give appropriate and sensitive feedback to a teacher.

CRITERIA FOR GOOD LECTURING

These are listed below in the form of questions that an observer might ask when observing teaching.

Mood

- Does the lecturer display an appropriate and professional attitude towards students?
- Does the lecturer introduce him/her self?

Context

- Is the topic introduced in a stimulating way?

- Is prior learning activated?
- Are connections made to previous lectures?
- Are the topic's importance and relevance stressed?
- Are the students motivated to learn?

Outcomes

- Are learning outcomes stated?
- Are they relevant and appropriate to the curriculum and to the level of the students?
- Are they achievable in the time available?
- Do they show a cognitive range?

Content

- Is there an appropriate amount of information presented in the time available?
- Is the information structured effectively?
- Does the lecturer help the students navigate through the content?
- Are the explanations clear and do they use a range of examples, images, and analogies?

Presentation skills

- Is the lecturer articulate and does he or she use a clear and well-modulated voice?
- If a white/blackboard is used is it used effectively and can students read what is written?
- If an overhead projector and acetates are used are acetates clearly visible, is the text an appropriate size, is handwriting legible?
- If PowerPoint is used are slides well organized and designed and do they use an appropriate font at an appropriate font size?
- Are other AV aids (video, computer animations etc.) competently incorporated into the presentation?
- Are any handouts clearly written and designed?

- If interactivity is used is it well managed and are students adequately primed and encouraged to participate?
- Does the lecturer demonstrate enthusiasm for the subject and is he or she stimulating and interesting?
- Is time managed well? Is the presentation well paced?

Closure

- Does the lecturer emphasize the conclusions and summarize the key points?
- Does the lecturer give the students a sense of accomplishment?

COMMON LECTURING PROBLEMS AND THEIR SOLUTIONS

Some common presentation problems are discussed below with suggestions for improvement.

Too much material

This is the commonest fault of lecturing. Novice lecturers routinely overestimate the amount of material they think they can present. They genuinely want to tell students about the things they think are important and they are reluctant to remove material. They also underestimate the amount of time it takes to explain concepts in a lecture. Taken together this results in poor time management, an increase in pace towards the end of the lecture, increased stress on students trying to keep up with note taking and the inability to finish the lecture in the time available. More importantly, by overwhelming students with information these lecturers actually inhibit the learning of key concepts.

Solution

Be ruthless about reducing the amount of material you wish to present. A lecture should be an expert overview, not a presentation of detail. Remember the slogan: 'Less is more'. Just because you 'cover' a topic doesn't mean students *learn* it. Use handouts with extra material and reading lists. Practise and time your presentation beforehand, particularly explanations that you might take for granted. Practise is nearly always faster than lecturing live. If you are concerned about having time over at the end, use it for engaging in questions.

No outcomes

This is another very common fault. Lecturers will tell students what they wish to cover in the lecture, thinking they are describing the outcomes. Outcomes are statements concerning what students *should be able to do* at the end of the lecture, not what information is covered. Sampled outcomes become assessment criteria and students need this information in order to focus their learning.

Solution

Think carefully about what you want students to be able to do after engaging with the material you cover. Do you want them to recall some factual information? Do you want them to be able to explain or describe things? Do you want them to be able to draw or to label diagrams? Do you want them to be able to derive or use a formula? Do you want them to compare and contrast evidence or critically evaluate theories? Appropriate lecture outcomes should be negotiated with the course coordinator. They should fit into the overall curriculum outcomes and should form the basis of sampled assessments.

No attempt at contextualization

Some lecturers just start straight into the content of the lecture without any introduction or attempt to make connections with prior knowledge or prior work, or without explaining why the topic is important. This can be confusing for students who may not have completely settled down or who fail to catch the significance of the lecture and see how it fits into the curriculum.

Solution

When starting a lecture always try to make connections with prior knowledge and explain the importance, relevance and usefulness of the topic.

Irrelevance

Occasionally a lecturer might deviate from the prescribed curriculum and teach material that, although interesting to the lecturer, is not in the syllabus and hence is technically irrelevant. This can also happen when lectures are given by outside lecturers or in lectures occurring during work experience when there is less central control over teaching.

Solution

Lecturing should be well coordinated centrally and peripherally and all lecturers should know the curriculum outcomes required in any given session.

Poor audio-visual aids

Some lecturers scribble indecipherably on whiteboards, blackboards or overhead transparencies. Some lecturers rub out material that is being copied down or else rub out sections of a formula or diagram and rewrite it, forgetting that the students have to rewrite all of it. Some users of PowerPoint use fonts that are too small and cram too much material onto one slide or else they use clashing colours and backgrounds that are difficult to read. Some lecturers insist on turning the lights off if showing slides or overheads when they can be perfectly well seen in normal lighting. This sends the audience to sleep and makes note taking difficult.

Solution

There is no excuse for poor handwriting in lectures. A lecture is about communication so ensure that writing is clear, neat and correctly spelled. Think about what you might write beforehand and plan how it might look. Remember that students may be trying to take notes so leave text up long enough for this activity and don't make changes that students can't adjust to. When using PowerPoint use a font size of at least 24; don't write all text in capital letters; preferably use a 'sans serif' font such as Arial or Comic Sans, and don't have coloured text clashing with coloured backgrounds. Keep it simple. Dimming or switching off the lights is usually not required with modern data projectors and good lighting keeps people awake and allows note taking.

Incompetent use of audio-visual aids

Sometimes lecturers arrive at the beginning of the lecture and are unable to operate the lights, the overhead projector, the computer or the data projector. They spend ten minutes fiddling about then ring the audio-visual unit technicians who are on call. Ten minutes later the lecture begins.

Solution

Always arrive early for a lecture using audio-visual aids and ensure all the equipment is working and you know how to use it. If there is a problem ring the AV technician on call straight away so it can be put right before the lecture is due to begin. Modern lecture theatres often have an integrated console that controls all the facilities. Make sure you know how to use it. Go there when the lecture theatre is not in use and practise using the equipment until you are fully competent and confident.

Poor explanations

During an explanatory sequence in a lecture the lecturer starts to 'um' and 'er' and jumps over sections too rapidly or without explanation. What is said does not appear to make logical sense. The lecturer realizes that he or she is not making a coherent and logical explanation.

Solution

Practise explanations until you are satisfied that you have a rational sequence that makes sense. Don't take your own understanding for granted and try to make up an explanation on the spot in a lecture, as it can go wrong. Just because you understand something doesn't mean you can explain it to someone who has never heard about it before.

Too fast

Lecturing too fast can be a result of too much content, as discussed above. However, it can also be the result of nervousness, when the lecturer wants to get the experience over with as quickly as possible.

Solution

Nerves have been dealt with in Chapter 3, but essentially the lecturer needs a good structure, with well-organized content and opportunities to practise and receive feedback from supportive colleagues.

Boring/monotonous/unstimulating

The lecturer speaks in a boring monotone. He or she uses the same presentation technique throughout the lecture with no variation. The material is presented in a very unstimulating way.

Solution

Practise modulating the voice. Go to a voice training class. Go on a teacher training course where good presentation techniques are demonstrated. Try to develop some enthusiasm for your subject!

LECTURING EVALUATION AND FEEDBACK

The criteria described above have been incorporated into a variety of checklists and protocols used to evaluate teachers. Although teachers can evaluate themselves it is also helpful to be evaluated either by a skilled teaching evaluator, by a colleague or peer, or else by students. Each of these methods has different biases and may use slightly different evaluation criteria. Race (2001) describes a variety of methods for obtaining feedback on lecturing.

External evaluation: the Quality Assurance Agency (QAA)

In the UK the QAA constitute an external and independent body that monitor and report on the quality of teaching in higher education. As

TABLE 10.1 QAA Teaching Observation form (I)

Observation note
(For use in teaching and learning sessions – both tutor-led sessions and students independent learning sessions)

Institution	Subject	Module/course unit
Reviewer	Session Length Hours Mins	Observation Hours Mins
Level/year	Mode, eg FT/PT	Number of students
Type of activity, eg lecture, CAL	Topic	Composition of the student group

What are the learning objectives planned for this session (eg knowledge and understanding, key skills, cognitive skills, and subject-specific, including practical/professional skills)?

Source: Subject Review Handbook: England and Northern Ireland (September 2000–December 2001); © Quality Assurance Agency for Education 2000

such during their visits to universities they have observed teaching and used a particular observation schedule and set of evaluative criteria. In particular QAA teaching evaluators were concerned with the clarity of the learning outcomes for each session they observe, with planning and organization, pace, content, interactivity and the use of learning resources. Although their methods have changed and evolved over the years it is useful to see the teaching evaluation forms they used during their visits. These are shown in Tables 10.1 and 10.2.

TABLE 10.2 QAA Teaching Observation form (II)

Please comment on strengths and weaknesses of the session in relation to the learning objectives

Prompts	Strengths	Weaknesses
Clarity of objectives Planning and organisation Methods/approach Delivery and pace Content (currency, accuracy, relevance, use of examples, level, match to student needs) Student participation Use of accommodation and learning resources		

Please summarise the session's overall quality in relation to the learning objectives

Please indicate relevance to other aspects

Source: Subject Review Handbook: England and Northern Ireland (September 2000–December 2001); © Quality Assurance Agency for Education 2000

Peer evaluation of teaching (PET)

PET schemes are set up within schools and departments and involve academics forming pairs or circles who observe, evaluate and feedback on each other's teaching during the academic year. The aim is to generate a community of teachers who are keen to improve their teaching,

TABLE 10.3 Peer evaluation of teaching

Name of presenter ....

Title of presentation ....

	Excellent	*Good*	*Fair*	*Poor*	*Very Poor*
	5	*4*	*3*	*2*	*1*
CONTEXT					
1. Introduction/Mood					
2. Motivation/Interest					
3. Clarity of Objectives					
CONTENT					
4. Structure/organization					
5. Explanation of Content					
6. Verbal delivery					
7. Time management					
8. Audio-visual aids					
9. Interactivity					
CLOSURE					
10. Summary/conclusions					
Column totals					
Total score					
% Score					

Comments: Strengths, weaknesses, improvements?

who are open to constructive criticism and who will use reflection to improve their practice. Ideally participants need to have been on a basic teacher training course so that they are familiar with the techniques of teaching and the criteria used to evaluate teachers. However, if that is not the case then they will meet beforehand to discuss the proposed teaching session, to share their views on good teaching and to agree appropriate criteria. They may use a checklist agreed by their school or department. The teacher might describe the overall structure and organization of the proposed session, its learning outcomes and any issues that require specific observation and feedback. In a developmentally focused teaching observation scheme it is very important that the teachers feel able to set the agenda and direct their observer's eye towards aspects of their teaching which they are keen to develop.

Observation of teaching may use a checklist similar to the one shown in Table 10.3.

After the session the observer and teacher should engage in a feedback discussion. A more detailed method of giving feedback will be discussed later but advice on giving general feedback in PET situations is provided below.

- Be realistic – direct your comments towards actions that your colleague can control.
- Be specific – generalizations are not helpful.
- Pinpoint something that your colleague can influence or change.
- Be sensitive to the goals of your colleague.
- Be consciously non-judgmental. Describe behaviour ('you interrupted three times'); don't judge people ('you are domineering').
- Be aware of balancing positive and negative feedback. Positive feedback on its own allows no room for improvement and negative feedback alone is discouraging.
- Be prompt – delay reduces impact.

(Adapted from Eastcott and Farmer 1992; O'Neill and Pennington 1992)

Teachers engaging in PET schemes also need to be aware of how to receive feedback.

- Be explicit – make it clear what kind of feedback you are seeking.
- Be aware – notice your own reactions, both intellectual and emotional.
- Be silent – you will hear more if you concentrate on listening rather than explaining or justifying yourself. Consciously try to avoid being defensive.
- Be clear – exactly what is your colleague saying to you? Ask for clarification if necessary; check understanding regularly.

(Adapted from Eastcott and Farmer 1992; O'Neill and Pennington 1992)

Teachers need to be aware that schools and departments may turn PET into a formally administered process involving forms and paperwork for the purposes of teaching quality enhancement and for providing evidence to the QAA that teaching evaluation and development is taking place. This is very important as in future most universities will be externally reviewed through a 'light touch' self-evaluation process.

Giving feedback to a teacher

In order for lecturers to improve they need feedback on their performance. However, feedback has to be constructive and given in a sensitive way to avoid any negative feelings that might inhibit development. Brief mention has been given above to feedback that might be provided on PET schemes. However, a more sophisticated method has been developed which manages to give helpful feedback in such a way that the receiver sees it as a positive experience (Pendleton *et al.* 1984). The overall process is designed to be learner-centred, starting from the experiences of the teacher. It involves discussing positive achievements, then dealing with problem areas, but providing helpful suggestions for improvement. The problems are sandwiched between positive observations and solutions, hence the name 'feedback sandwich'.

Assuming the evaluator has observed the teacher's lecture they might then sit down together afterwards. The first thing the evaluator does is to ask the teacher what he or she thought was positive or worked well in the lecture. Note that they are starting from the lecturer's experience and concentrating on the positive. Experience shows that 99 times out of 100 if you ask teachers how their session went they will immediately start talking about the negative.

Hopefully the lecturer will give positive descriptions or evaluations of his or her performance. The evaluator should next reinforce these with any further positive personal observations.

Next the evaluator asks the lecturer what might be done differently given any problems he or she encountered during the presentation. Note that the lecturer is not necessarily being asked to dwell on problems but rather to think of solutions.

After listening to the lecturer's possible solutions the evaluator can start to make further helpful suggestions. In addition, if the evaluator has spotted further problems that the lecturer might have been unaware of, he or she can mention them, emphasizing possible solutions the lecturer might like to consider.

In summary the process should go like this:

1. Ask the lecturer to describe his or her positive achievements:

   'Tell me what you thought went well in your presentation.'

2. Respond positively and if possible describe further examples of good teaching techniques you have observed:

   'I agree. I liked the way you . . . And I also liked . . .'

3. Ask the teacher to describe how he or she might deal with any problem areas encountered during the presentation:

   'Are there any things you would do differently given any problems you may have encountered during the lecture?'

4. Add your own suggestions for dealing with problems and for improving practice:

   'Yes, but why don't you try . . . Try concentrating more on . . . Next time you can . . . It might be useful to . . . Have you thought of . . .'

Student evaluation of teaching

There is a certain logic to the idea that students should evaluate the teaching they are subjected to since in one sense they are the consumers and teachers are the producers. However, the precise relationship between teachers and students depends on a variety of variables ranging from the student's understanding of what teaching is to the teacher's understanding of what learning is. For example, students might think that teaching is merely the transmission of factual information in didactic lectures whereas teachers might think that learning is an active process of personal construction requiring student interaction and responsibility. There is considerable scope for potential misunderstanding between these two extremes and it is important to recognize the biases that might exist on both sides. Nevertheless, most teachers can obtain something for their own personal benefit by asking a few simple questions of students at the end of a teaching session and a variety of formal Student Evaluation of Teaching schemes have also been produced.

A simple feedback questionnaire containing open-ended questions, which might be given to students after a presentation or lecture, might contain the following:

- What did you find most useful about that lecture?
- What did you find least useful about that lecture?
- What did you find interesting?
- What did you find difficult?
- What improvements could be made to the lecture?

TABLE 10.4 A student evaluation of teaching questionnaire generated by a central system (University of Nottingham)

Seven questions standard for all questionnaires:

1. Is this module compulsory for you?
2. Have you attended at least 80% of the sessions timetabled for you with this teacher?

Questions 1 and 2 are answered as either yes or no by the respondent.

3. The teacher was an able communicator
4. The teacher retained my interest
5. The teacher was approachable
6. Sessions were paced appropriately
7. Overall, this teacher assisted my learning

Questions 3 to 7 are answered by the respondent ticking a box indicating one of the following six categories; N/A, strongly agree, agree, neutral, disagree, strongly disagree.

This is followed by a set of subject specific questions (a variety of which are shown below) with the same rating categories as questions 3–7.

1. The aims and objectives were clear
2. I could hear the lecture clearly
3. The teaching methods employed were appropriate to the subject matter
4. The lecture material was well structured
5. The subject matter was developed logically
6. The teacher related the subject matter to practice and current available evidence
7. The teacher stimulated my interest in the subject
8. The teacher encouraged me to think and question during the lecture
9. The explanations given by the teacher were clear
10. The teacher emphasized key points
11. The teacher pointed out links to previous topics we have studied
12. The visual aids used were clear and helped me understand the lecture
13. The teacher adopted a professional attitude
14. The teacher was approachable
15. The teacher treated me with respect
16. Prior reading/preparation was relevant and well organized
17. The teacher exercised fairness in time and attention to both sides of the debate
18. The teacher demonstrated an awareness of students with special needs
19. The teacher corrects errors without causing embarrassment

Another simple system suggested by Race (2001) is to ask students:

- what should be stopped
- what should be started
- what should be continued.

University-based Student Evaluation of Teaching systems can generate checklists containing a great variety of criteria which might be more useful for particular disciplines. These can combine generic criteria with subject-specific criteria on one form to be used by students. An example is shown in Table 10.4.

FURTHER READING

Blackwell, R. and McLean, M. (1996) Peer observation of teaching and staff development, *HE Quarterly*, 50(2): 156–71.

Brown, S., Jones, G. and Rawnsley, S. (eds) (1993) *Observing Teaching*, SEDA Paper 79, p. 96. Birmingham: Staff and Educational Development Association.

Eastcott, D. and Farmer, R. (1992) Planning Teaching for Active Learning, Module 3, *Effective Learning and Teaching in Higher Education*. Sheffield: Committee of Vice-Chancellors and Principals/Universities' Staff Development and Training Unit.

O'Neill, M. and Pennington, G. (1992) *Evaluating Teaching and Programmes from an Active Learning Perspective*. London: Committee of Vice-Chancellors and Principals.

USEFUL WEB SITES

http://www.lgu.ac.uk/deliberations/forum/peer-obs.html The *Deliberations* website provides a wide range of teaching articles, discussions and links and has a useful section of resources on Peer Observation of Teaching: *Can Peer Observation Improve Teaching? If So, How Should It Be Done?*

http://www.ltsn.ac.uk/application.asp?app=resources.asp&process=full_record&section=generic&id=200 Gosling, D. (2002) *Models of Peer Observation of Teaching*. York: Learning and Teaching Support Network Generic Centre. Teaching Quality Enhancement Fund National Coordination Team.

http://www.ltsn.ac.uk/genericcentre/index.asp?id=17849 The generic centre project on Peer Observation of Teaching (POT) provides links to further resources and support for new teachers as well as information about POT.

http://www.wisc.edu/provost/ccae/MOO/ Peer Review of Teaching (PRoT) site at the University of Wisconsin, Madison provides guidance on using peer observation as a process for improving your teaching and on how it can be used to show evidence of good teaching.

Different university schemes, guidance and information

Several universities have set up peer observation schemes and written handbooks and provided guidance on the subject. These include examples of proformas and checklists to assist in the observation process and in giving feedback to peers on their teaching. For example:

Centre for Educational Development at Imperial College, London:
http://www.ic.ac.uk/icced/OpenLearning/peerobservation2.htm

University of Leicester:
http://www.le.ac.uk/staffdev/advice_procedures_forms/observation_of_teaching.html

University of Nottingham:
http://www.nottingham.ac.uk/sedu/peerobs/
and http://www.nottingham.ac.uk/pgche/environment/peerobs.php

University of Reading:
http://www.rdg.ac.uk/Handbooks/Teaching_and_Learning/Peer_Review_Guidelines.html

University of Southampton:
http://www.artsnet.soton.ac.uk/learning_teaching/peerobservation/

LTSN subject centre and discipline-specific peer observation links

Several of the Learning and Teaching Support Network (LTSN) subject centres have provided more discipline-specific guidance on teaching observation. For example:

Education Subject Centre, Escalate:
http://www.escalate.ac.uk/exchange/PeerReview/

DEVELOP (Developing Excellence in Language Teaching through the Observation of Peers) is a three-year FDTL 2 project funded by HEFCE. This site includes resources and information generated specifically with the language teacher in mind – however, the materials on giving and receiving feedback are very useful for all teachers.
http://www.ncteam.ac.uk/projects/fdtl/fdtl2/projectdescriptions/42-97.htm

Liz Beaty and Ian McGill have developed a video training pack, *Observation for Reflective Practice*. It contains a video case study and a package of OHTs, preparatory materials and handouts, etc., to help a staff developer run a workshop of up to one day. It can be purchased through Martin Hayden, Head of Learning Resources, Brighton University.

Appendix 1 An outline of the legal position with regard to supporting students with disabilities

THE LEGAL POSITION: SUPPORTING DISABLED STUDENTS (taken from Exley and Dennick 2004, originally adapted from guidance provided by the Disability Rights Commission)

From September 2002, the Disability Discrimination Act (DDA) 1995 (as amended by the Special Educational Needs and Disability Act (SENDA) 2001) makes it unlawful for providers of education and related services to discriminate against disabled people.

In law the college or university is responsible for both the actions of:

- full-time and part-time employees of the institution in the course of their employment, and
- external and visiting speakers, etc.

However, individual teachers and tutors may also be held responsible for aiding an unlawful act if they knowingly discriminate against a disabled student.

The Act uses a wide definition of disabled person and institutions are expected to take reasonable steps to find out if a person is disabled. It can include people with:

- physical or mobility impairments
- visual and hearing impairments
- dyslexia and dyspraxia

- medical conditions, and
- mental health difficulties.

There are two ways in which a tutor could discriminate against a disabled student:

- treating them 'less favourably' than other people, or
- failing to make a 'reasonable adjustment' when, because of their disability, they are placed at a 'substantial disadvantage' when compared to other students.

The Act applies to all the activities and facilities institutions provide wholly or mainly for students, including, for example:

- all aspects of teaching and learning, including, SGT, lectures, lab work, practicals, field trips, etc.
- e-learning, distance learning and teaching resources
- examinations and assessments
- learning resources, including libraries, computer facilities, etc.

From the lecturer's point of view the main focus of the legislation is the clear need to make **anticipatory reasonable adjustments** to the teaching, learning and assessment approaches used in order to make the learning experience accessible to all students.

Exactly what might constitute a reasonable adjustment will depend on the needs of the students, the requirements and academic standards of the course, the resources of the institution and the practicality of the adjustment (including its impact on other students). In general terms a reasonable adjustment might be any action that helps to alleviate a substantial disadvantage, for example:

- changing institutional procedures
- adapting the curriculum, making adaptations to electronic or other materials used by the student, or modifying the delivery of teaching
- providing additional services, such as a sign language interpreter or materials in large font or Braille
- raising awareness and training staff to work with disabled people
- making modifications to the physical environment.

'Anticipatory' adjustments means that universities (and teachers) should consider what adjustments future disabled students may need, and make them in advance. The QAA Code of Practice for students with disabilities recommends:

TABLE A1.1 The QAA Code of Practice for Students with Disabilities recommendation

Precept 10.

The delivery of programmes should take into account the needs of disabled people, or, where appropriate, be adapted to accommodate their individual requirements. Institutions should consider making arrangements which ensure that all academic staff and technical staff;

- Plan and employ teaching and learning strategies which make the delivery of the programme as inclusive as possible;
- Know and understand the learning implications of any disabilities of their student whom they teach and are responsive to student feedback;
- Make individual adaptations to delivery that are appropriate for particular students.

The Disability Rights Commission is offering a conciliation service for students and institutions to reconcile any differences informally. If both parties do not agree to conciliation, or if conciliation fails, a student or applicant can take a case to a county court (in England or Wales) or a Sheriff court (in Scotland).

Confidentiality

Universities are expected to take reasonable steps to find out about a student's disability. Once the university is aware that a student has a disability, either because it is obvious (e.g. visible) or the student has disclosed it, the institution has a responsibility not to discriminate. It is worth remembering that if a student tells his or her tutor that they have a disability then, in the eyes of the law, the student has informed the university.

Students do, of course, have a right to confidentiality, both through the Data Protection Act and separately within the Disability Discrimination Act. However, for some courses there may be a particular health and safety requirement that means disabled students are required to disclose certain disabilities for the safety of themselves and others.

Appendix 2 Additional sources of information on specific disabilities and support organizations

Organization	*Contact details*
Action for M.E.	www.afme.org.uk
Association for Spina Bifida and Hydrocephalus (ASBAH)	www.asbah.org.uk
British Council of Disabled People	www.bcodp.org.uk
The National Autistic Society	www.nas.org.uk
British Dyslexia Association	www.bda-dyslexia.org.uk
Epilepsy Action	www.epilepsy.org.uk
Dyspraxia Foundation	www.emmbrook.demon.co.uk/dysprax/what.htm
Mental Health Foundation	www.mentalhealth.org.uk
MIND	www.mind.org.uk
O.A.S.I.S. (on-Line Asperger's Syndrome Information Resources)	www.udel.edu/bkirby/asperger/index.html
Royal National Institute for Deaf People	www.rnid.org.uk
Royal National Institute for the Blind	www.rnib.org.uk
SKILL: National Bureau for students with disabilities	www.skill.org.uk

Organization	*Contact details*
TechDis (For information on making electronic materials accessible)	www.techdis.ac.uk
University students with Autism and Asperger's Syndrome	www.users.dircon.co.uk/~cns/index.html

References

Andreson, L. (1994) *Lecturing to Large Groups*, SEDA Paper 81. Birmingham: Staff and Educational Development Association.

Ausubel, D. (1968) *Educational Psychology: A Cognitive View*. New York, NY: Holt, Rinehart and Winston.

Barker, H., McLean, M. and Roseman, M. (2000) 'Re-thinking the history curriculum: enhancing students' communication and group-work skills', in A. Booth and P. Hyland, *The Practice of University History Teaching*. Manchester: Manchester University Press.

Baume, D. and Baume, C. (1996) *Learning to Teach: Making Presentations*, Training Materials for Research Students. Oxford: Oxford Centre for Staff Development.

Biggs, J. (1999a) 'Enriching large-class teaching', in *Teaching for Quality Learning at University*. Buckingham: Society for Research into Higher Education and Open University Press.

Biggs, J. (1999b) *Teaching for Quality Learning at University*. Buckingham: Society for Research into Higher Education and Open University Press.

Blicharski, J. R. D. (1999) 'New undergraduates: access and helping them prosper', *Widening Participation And Lifelong Learning*, The Journal of The Institute for Access Studies and The European Access Network, 1(1).

Bligh, D. (1998) *What's the Use of Lectures*, 2nd edition. Exeter: Intellect Press.

Blix, A. G., Cruise, R. J., Mitchell, B. M. and Blix, G. G. (1994) 'Occupational stress among university teachers', *Educational Research*, 36(2): 157–69.

Bloom, B. S. (1956 and 1964) *Taxonomy of Educational Objectives*, 2 vols. New York, NY: Longmans Green.

Bonwell, C. C. and Eison, J. A. (1991) *Active Learning: Creating Excitement in the Classroom*, ASHE-ERIC Higher Education Report No. 1. Washington, DC: George Washington University, School of Education and Human Development.

Boyle, J. T. and Nicol, D. J. (2003) 'Using classroom communication systems to support interaction and discussion in large class settings', *Association of Learning Technology Journal*, 11(3): 43–57.

Brown, G. (2004) *How Students Learn*. http://routledgefalmer.com/series/KGETHE.

Brown, G. and Manogue, M. (2001) *Refreshing Lecturing: A Guide for Lecturers*. AMEE Medical Education Guide No. 22, *Medical Teacher*, 23(3): 231–44.

Brown, G. A. and Atkins, M. J. (1988) *Effective Teaching in Higher Education*. London: Routledge.

Bruner, J. (1968) *Towards a Theory of Instruction*. New York, NY: Norton.

Butler, J. A. (1992) 'Use of teaching methods within the lecture format', *Medical Teacher*, 14(1), 11–23.

Carville, S. and Mitchell, D. R. (2000) 'It's a bit like Star Trek': the effectiveness of video conferencing, *Innovations in Education and Training International*, 37(1): 43–9.

Chin, P. (2004) *Using C&IT to Support Teaching*, London: RoutledgeFalmer.

Crowe, C. and Pemberton, A. (2000) *Interactive Lecturing with Large Classes: Students' Experiences and Performance in Assessment*. University of Queensland, Teaching and Educational Development Institute. http://www.tedi.uq.edu.au/conferences/teach_conference00/titles.html

Doyle, C. and Robson, K. (2001) *Accessible Curricula: Good Practice for All*. Cardiff: University of Wales. http://www.uwic.ac.uk/ltsu/accessible.pdf

Draper, S. (2003) *Using Handsets at Glasgow University*. http://www.psy.gla.ac.uk/~steve/ilig/local.html#intro

Dufresne, R. J., Gerace, W. J., Leonard, W. J., Mestre, J. P. and Wenk, L. (1996) 'Classtalk: a classroom communication system for active learning', *Journal of Computing in Higher Education*, 7: 3–47.

Eastcott, D. and Farmer, R. (1992) Planning Teaching for Active Learning, Module 3, *Effective Learning and Teaching in Higher Education*. Sheffield: Committee of Vice-Chancellors and Principals/Universities' Staff Development and Training Unit.

Edwards, H., Smith, B. and Webb, G. (eds) (2001) *Lecturing: Case Studies, Experience and Practice*. London: Kogan Page.

Exley, K. and Dennick, R. (2004) *Small Group Teaching*. London: RoutledgeFalmer.

Farmer, M., Riddick, B. and Sterling, C. (2002) *Dyslexia and Inclusion: Assessment and Support in Higher Education*. London: Whurr.

Gardner, H. (1993) *Multiple Intelligences: The Theory in Practice*. New York, NY: Basic Books.

Gardner, L. E. and Leak, G. K. (1994) 'Characteristics and correlates of teaching anxiety among college psychology teachers', *Teaching of Psychology*, 21(1): 28–32.

Hayton, A. and Paczuska, A. (eds) (2002) *Participation and Higher Education*. London: Kogan Page.

HEFCE (Higher Education Funding Council for England) (2001) *Strategies for Learning and Teaching in Higher Education*, Report 01/37, http://www.hefce.ac.uk/pubs/hefce/2001/01_37.htm

HEFCE (2003) *Supporting Higher Education in Further Education Colleges: A Guide for Tutors and Lecturers*, Report 03/15. http://www.hefce.ac.uk/pubs/hefce/2003/03_15.htm

Hinton, B. and Manathuuga, C. (2001) 'The mobile phone', in H. Edwards, B. Sunim and G. Webb (eds) *Lecturing: Case Studies, Experience and Practice*. London: Kogan Page.

Honey, P. and Mumford, A. (1982) *The Manual of Learning Styles*. Available from Peter Honey. http://www.peterhoney.co.uk/main

Johnstone, A. H. and Parcival, F. (1976) 'Attention breaks in lectures', *Education in Chemistry*, 13(2): 48–50.

Johnstone, A. H. and Su, W. Y. (1994) 'Lectures: a learning experience', *Education in Chemistry*, 31(3): 75–9.

Jung, C. G. and Baynes, H. G. (1971) *Psychological Types*. Revision by R. F. C. Hull of the translation by H. G. Baynes, Bollingen Series XX. Princeton, NJ: Princeton University Press.

Keirsey, D. (1998) *Please Understand Me: Character and Temperament Types*. Del Mar, CA: Prometheus Nemesis Book Company.

Kolb, D. A. (1984) *Experiential Learning*. Englewood Cliffs, NJ: Prentice-Hall.

Lee, A. Y. and Bowers, A. N. (1997) *The Effect of Multimedia Components on Learning*, Proceedings of the Human Factors and Ergonomics Society 41st Annual Meeting. http://www.humanfactors.com/downloads/july98.asp

Lucas, R. W. (2000) *The Big Book of Flip Charts: A Comprehensive Guide for Presenters, Trainers and Team Facilitators*. New York, NY: McGraw-Hill.

MacNevin, A. L. (2000) *Effective Lecturing and the Use of Body Language*. Saint Mary's University, Halifax, Nova Scotia, Department of Sociology, TDC Newsletter. http://www.uregina.ca/tdc/EffectLect

Mason, J. H. (2002) *Mathematics Teaching Practice: Guide for University and College Lecturers*. Chichester: Harwood Publishing.

Mazur, E. (1997) *Peer Instruction: A User's Manual*. New Jersey, NJ: Prentice-Hall.

Myers, I. B. and Briggs, K. C. (2002) *Myers-Briggs Type Indicator*. http://www.cppdb.com/products/mbti/index.asp

Nicol, D. J. and Boyle, J. T. (2003) 'Peer instruction versus class-wide discussion in large classes: a comparison of two interaction methods in the wired classroom', *Studies in Higher Education*, 28(4): 457–73.

O'Neill, M. and Pennington, G. (1992) *Evaluating Teaching and Programmes from an Active Learning Perspective*. London: Committee of Vice-Chancellors and Principals.

Pendleton, D., Schofield, T., Tate, P. and Havelock, P. (1984) *The Consultation: An Approach to Learning and Teaching*. Oxford: Oxford University Press.

Piaget, J. (1969) *Science of Education and the Psychology of the Child*. London: Longman.

Pitcher, N., Davidson, K. and Goldfinch, J. (2000) 'Videoconferencing in higher education', *Innovations in Education and Training International*, 37(3): 199–209.

QAA (Quality Assurance Agency for Higher Education) (1999) Code of Practice for the Assurance of Academic Quality and Standards in Higher Education: Students with Disabilities. http://www.qaa.ac.uk/public/COP/COPswd/contents.htm

QAA (Quality Assurance Agency for Higher Education) (2000) *Guidelines on Preparing Programme Specifications*. http://www.qaa.ac.uk/crntwork/progspec/prog-spec-contents_textonly.htm

QAA (Quality Assurance Agency for Higher Education) (2003) A brief guide to quality assurance in UK higher education http://www.qaa.ac.uk/public/heguide/guide.htm

Race, P. (1999) *2000 Tips for Lecturers*. London: Kogan Page.

Race, P. (2001) *The Lecturer's Tool Kit*, 2nd edition. London: Kogan Page.

Russel, I. J., Hendricson, W. D. and Herbert, R. J. (1984) 'Effects of lecture information density on medical student achievement', *Journal of Medical Education*, 59(1): 881–9.

Sherin, N. (1995) *Oxford Dictionary of Humorous Quotations*. Oxford: Oxford University Press.

Somers, K. D. and Campbell, A. E. (1996) 'The lecture duet: an innovative technique to promote interactive learning in a traditional lecture-based curriculum', in K. Exley and R. Dennick (eds) *Innovations in Teaching Medical Sciences*, SEDA Paper 93. Birmingham: SEDA.

Springer, S. P. and Deutsch, G. (1993) *Left Brain/Right Brain*, 4th edition. New York, NY: W.H. Freeman.

Stefani, L. (2001) 'We might have to learn it but we shouldn't have to think about it', in H. Edwards, B. Smith and G. Webb (eds) *Lecturing: Case Studies, Experience and Practice*. London: Kogan Page.

SWANDS (South West Academy Network for Disability Support) (2002) 'Preparing documents', in *SENDA Compliance in Higher Education*, SWANDS Project, University of Plymouth. http://www.plym.ac.uk/pages/view.asp?page=3243

TA Handbook (2002) *Disruptive Students*. The University of Delaware: Centre for Teaching Effectiveness. http://www.udel.edu/cte/TAbook/disruptive.html

University of New South Wales (1991) *Code of Practice – Students with Disabilities*. Sydney, Australia. http://www.equity.unsw.edu.au/codeofpr.html

University of California, Santa Cruz, *The Instructors' Guidelines for Addressing Disruptive Students in the Classroom*, http://www2.ucsc.edu/sadiv/disrupt.stu.html

Vygotsky, L. (1978) *Mind in Society: The Development of Higher Psychological Processes*. Cambridge, MA: Harvard University Press.

Waterfield, J. and West, B. (2002) *SENDA Compliance in Higher Education*. Plymouth: South West Academic Network for Disability Support (SWANDS).

Williams, E. (1992) 'Student attitudes towards approaches to learning and assessment', *Assessment and Evaluation in Higher Education*, 17(1): 45–58.

Yoshinaga-Itano, C. (2002) *Diversity, Individual Difference and Students with Disabilities: Optimising the Learning Environment*. http://www.colorado.edu/ftep/diversity/div13.html

Index

Page numbers in *italics* refer to figures and tables, *a* indicates appendix.